This book is dedicated to Betty and David Segalov, who taught me the importance of community and compassion. And to Tamir, who will carry that into the future.

ACTIVISM
Teen
361.2
Segalov
2018

Published in 2018 by Laurence King Publishing Ltd

361–373 City Road
London EC1V 1LR
Tel: +44 20 7841 6900
Fax: +44 20 7841 6910
Email: enquiries@laurenceking.com
www.laurenceking.com

A catalog record for this book is available from the British Library.

ISBN: 978-1-78627-206-5

Art direction and design: Oliver Stafford, TCO London
Cover design: Mylène Mozas, mylenemozas.com

Printed in China

RESIST!

How to be an Activist in the Age of Defiance

Michael Segalov

Laurence King Publishing

CONTENTS

—

FOREWORD
BY MOLLY CRABAPPLE
—

Before I get into the urgent necessity of this book, let's start with some memories.

The night I sat with a group of friends on the plastic sheets, spread out over my living room, painting signs for May Day. We had scrounged the cardboard from the trash, then worked out an assembly line, cutting each rectangle neatly, painting it crimson, front and back, then carefully lettering our slogans in Spanish, Yiddish, Persian, English, Arabic.

We drank whiskey in between, till our heads spun and dawn filtered through the window, and then I dragged the signs to our group's appointed meeting place the next morning, where fifty people showed up, and we carried the signs down Broadway—now a sea of unmistakable, triumphant red.

The morning I was arrested at a demonstration. Remembering those know-your-rights pamphlets,

I asked the officer if I could leave, and wisely shut up when he told me I could not, except to shout my name, as I'd seen other people being arrested do.

The protesters around me shouted it, and it echoed back, through the crowd, until someone who knew me heard it, and told my friends, who were waiting for me when I was released, sixteen hours later.

The countless meetings, long and dull and necessary, where we learned who was in charge of the particular sliver of bureaucracy that now permitted immigration officers to go into courthouses, where they dragged people without papers off to detention—which might mean exile or death.

The DC courtroom, at the trial of five people—out of 194—who had been arrested protesting Trump's inauguration. The prosecutor with the pinched

face of Cruella de Vil brought out a
bag containing the defendant's belongings,
and held each piece in her rubber gloved hand.
She displayed them nakedly, these fragments of
protest culture, now stripped of context. Jail
support forms; a roll of gauze; rags soaked in
vinegar in a ziplock bag (a DIY remedy against
tear gas). Her mouth thin, she told the jury
these objects were proof that the protesters
had planned a riot. The jury declared the
protesters innocent.

The time demonstrators shut down a highway,
and I followed them. They stood, their bodies
daring the cars, the city twinkling behind them
in bright, bitter fragments of light.

Protest is many things. Romance. Habit.
A necessity, in these times of fascism, closing
borders, and malignant shouty stupid. But
what these memories illustrate is that protest
is above all a set of practices. And at this

moment, when the world is moving fast, and the consequences growing ever graver, these are practices that everyone has got to learn.

And this is why this new book is so crucial. We need to fight hard, and well, with all the tools at our disposal. Sometimes, this looks like painting banners, or disrupting planes deporting refugees, or figuring out the exact person in charge of the exact bit of skullduggery that's ruining lives on your block.

And these are the skills this book has to teach. It is something that could be called a recipe book, a compilation of troublemaking techniques and rebel lore, beautifully packaged, and filled with sharp words from activists well-known and not.

It's easy to look at the black and white pictures of the people who demonstrated against apartheid, or who linked arms in the Miners'

Strike, and think they are fundamentally different than us.

But they are humans, who got the same number of hours in each day that we do, who employed specific methods to fight specific fights. They also put up posters and got paint under their nails and froze in police kettles. They too had to learn, night by night, meeting by meeting, skills for rebellion and survival.

So, read about how to drop a banner, design a placard, further your cause through social media, support your jailed friends.

"GET STRONGER.
GET BETTER.
GET DANGEROUS."

INTRODUCTION
—

As children we want to be great leaders—to embark on journeys through uncharted territory, and to charge headfirst with boundless energy and limitless dreams into the world that sits before us. A bright vision of the future seems to sit in the palm of our little hands.

It's not long, though, before we're pounded with "reality" from every direction—slammed doors and sceptical looks wherever we turn. We're told that there's no point trying to build something better; that one day we'll grow up, grow compliant, grow tired of wanting something more. "That's life," we're told.

But the first lesson that any activist needs to learn is that it doesn't have to be this way. When Rosa Parks refused to move to the back of the bus, when the Pankhursts led the suffragettes on their hunger strikes, when the Stonewall rioters refused to apologize for being gay—they looked around and saw possibility.

For those who continue to see possibility around them, this book aims to provide the tools to follow in the footsteps of these pioneers.

Today we are faced with a world that feels increasingly fragmented and hostile. Our futures seem less certain than ever before.

The challenges we face are far-reaching and, at times, feel insurmountable: climate change, the rise of bigotry, international conflict, and the widening gap between the richest and the poorest are just the tip of the iceberg.

That's not to say it's time to resign ourselves to a future of hatred and destruction. Quite the opposite. Now is the time to fight back. We live in the age of resistance. From the local to the international, a collective consciousness is forming. It's up to you to play your part.

Some look at the world around them and feel emboldened to take action, while others are pushed to the brink and left feeling that they have little choice but to act. It doesn't matter how you get there—what matters is that you take a stand. We have no other choice.

Change happens when ordinary people do extraordinary things. There's no National Society of Activists, no certificate that will qualify you to fight for a cause, but the pages that follow cover all the basics you need to know. From the arts of petitioning and protesting to how to articulate your message and how to get it heard, this book will be your guide. It will explore how to harness the power of the internet, hold effective meetings, and build a movement that can take on a life of its own.

Whether you want to stand proudly at the back of a million-strong march or be the one at the front wielding the megaphone, the tips, tricks, and stories that follow should provide ample inspiration to accompany you on your journey.

It doesn't matter if you're a seasoned activist or just getting started. One approach alone is unlikely to lead to success; utilizing a range of tactics is your best chance of victory. Change takes both time and persistence: the foundations of a new world are evolving every minute of every day.

And a final, important note. This book is not encouraging you to break the law. But democracy has a long and noble tradition of peaceful disobedience—and sometimes, protesting for what's right can result in the letter of the law being infringed. If do you encounter gray areas, just remember: never, ever use threats or violence.

THE STAKES ARE FAR TOO HIGH.

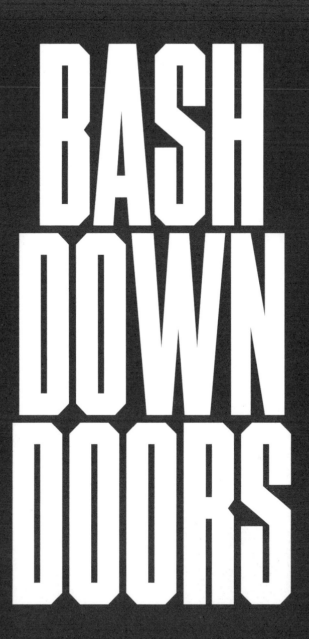

BASH DOWN DOORS

How to talk to people in power

INTRODUCTION
—

It's not hard to find reasons to be angry, especially when injustice is everywhere you turn. Feeling fired up and ready for action is the starter's mark in your race to changing the world for the better, and identifying who has the power to make those changes happen is the first step on your campaign's journey to the finish line.

Power doesn't rest with just one office, ballot box, or boardroom: it's not just leaders at the highest level of government who have the authority to listen and take action. Change is seldom sparked by a single person, either. Instead, we're influenced by those around us who shape our actions as they follow their course. Sometimes your focus will be local; at other times you'll want to tell the whole world about your plans for a better tomorrow.

Who has the power to make a change?

Start off by digging deep into the issue you've identified as important. Research all you can about that topic. Scour the Internet, open up a history book and don't be afraid to contact activists you find online for advice. Sometimes working out whose minds need changing will be easy, but at other times a complex web will quickly form.

Whether it's the closure of a local library that has you seething, a supermarket selling unethical products, or the government leading your country to war, mapping out where power lies will will be invaluable to your cause.

Creating a campaign to win is no mean feat, but if you haven't identified who has the power to bring about change, you might well find yourself targeting your efforts in the wrong direction.

Let's say you want the cost of rent reduced in your college dorm rooms. Do you speak to a class representative, your lecturer, the cleaning staff, the student council, or the company responsible for maintaining the building?

Power mapping is a tool you can use to identify your targets. It isn't just about picking out who sits at the table, but who they are influenced by, and what might matter to them. This is an exercise in unpicking power dynamics—identifying the different stakeholders, as well as the various levels of power and how they intersect. In every power map there will be both primary and secondary targets: the people who'll have the final say, and those who can put pressure on them.

Power mapping in 10 easy steps

1 | Start off by identifying the problem you believe needs fixing, and get a rounded understanding of the forces with a vested interest in it.

2 | Next, it's time for some serious research. Identify the main stakeholders. Try asking yourself:

- Who is responsible for creating the problem?
- Who has the power to fix the problem?
- Who has a personal relationship with the issue?
- Who lives locally and is affected?
- Which companies or organizations are involved already?
- Who might support you but isn't yet involved?
- Who is already working to try and fix things?
  (Don't forget to include your own group in the list.)

3 | Within the institutions and organizations you've identified there'll be specific people with power—individuals who can bring about change. Create a list of these names.

4 | Take your list and ask yourself two questions: do these people agree or disagree with you on the issue, and how much power do they really hold?

5 | Draw the diagram opposite on a large piece of paper. Write the names you've collated onto sticky notes and then plot them on the graph.

6 | It's now time to scope out your primary target—the individual you've identified as having the most influence and who is also likely to give you what you want. In an ideal world your perfect target would be the most powerful and the most sympathetic; however, in reality these rarely go hand in hand. If there isn't one clear winner, or you have the capacity to take on more, try the next step with a selection of individuals. Remove the sticky notes naming your chosen target(s) from the chart, then proceed.

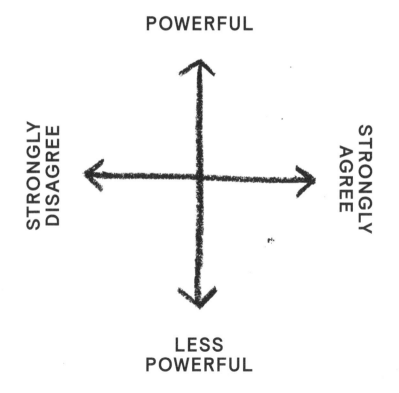

POWERFUL

STRONGLY
DISAGREE

STRONGLY
AGREE

LESS
POWERFUL

7 | You will now create your power map. Grab another large piece of paper and stick down your chosen sticky notes detailing the various people and organizations involved. Then map the power relations that connect your primary target(s). Do this by drawing links between other stakeholders you've previously identified and your primary target, and add new names into the mix where relevant, too. It sounds like a complex task, but when you put pen to paper it'll be easier than you think. Use arrows to map out the nexus—and don't forget to include your own group and any potential relationships you can build.

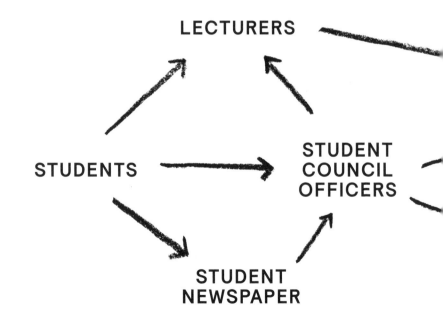

8 | Now repeat the process with the secondary targets on your power map by drawing around their names. It might not always be possible to reach your primary target directly—or even those whom they'll be influenced by—so the broader your network of potential access points, the better.

9 | Your completed power map now offers a logical plan for how to reach your target. You should be able to identify who can give you what you want, not just those who are easiest to reach.

10 | Revisit this process as your campaign develops. As you immerse yourself in the issue, new names, faces, and relationships might well come to the fore.

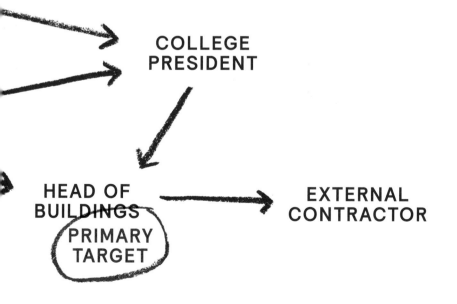

COLLEGE
PRESIDENT

HEAD OF
BUILDINGS
PRIMARY
TARGET

EXTERNAL
CONTRACTOR

Talking to politicians

Protest and activism are the lifeblood of any democracy, but politicians at every level can be vital in helping to further support for a cause. Elected officials in your local county, township, or municipality should be your go-to people for campaigns in your community. State Governors and state Senators have the power to effect change locally, and can help champion your ideas. Members of Congress and the Senate in Washington, DC will be prime targets for campaigns on a bigger scale.

We might not go to the polls very frequently to elect our representatives, but engaging with politicians should by no means be an activity that only takes place every few years. Your representatives have a responsibility to engage with their constituents, and they can be useful in a host of ways.

Securing a meeting with your Senator or Congressperson will take some organizing, but it's a powerful way of exerting your influence. Contacting their offices (either local or in DC) should be your starting point, their staff will have access to their diary and can let you know when they'll be in town. A short, simple letter or e-mail requesting a meeting should then follow, outlining who you are, why you want to meet, and your personal details.

You might ask your representative to put pressure on their party to throw their weight behind the campaign you're working on. Or if you know another politician who has an interest in your issue, get in touch with them.

FYI
—
To find the name and contact details of your local representatives, use the search function on the usa.gov/elected-officials website.

Ask yourself: why should they care?

While politicians and elected officials will have ideologies of their own, as well as party lines to follow and a desire to be reelected, private companies and corporations might care more about their bottom line. When you plan your approach for convincing different targets, make your case by speaking to them on their terms—but without watering down your position.

A supermarket chain wasting food at the end of every day might be immoral, but if you want them to donate leftovers to charity, it may be bad for their reputation if they refuse.

A Web search is the best way to identify who makes key decisions in private companies and organizations. Writing directly to the CEO is worth the effort, but being persistent might be the only way to ensure they take note. Sometimes just turning up at their HQ and demanding a meeting can pay off.

Get your facts straight

Employing research and statistics will help make your case to both the public and to decision-makers. Some people in power react most to having their heartstrings pulled, while others will be concerned solely with the cold hard facts. There's no harm in appealing to both the head and the heart.

Always double-check and cross-reference any information you stumble upon on the Internet. There's nothing worse than coming unstuck in a meeting or having your campaign's integrity undermined. Remember, though, that simple messages and storytelling are more important than stats. And don't be afraid to speak from personal experience.

Nothing beats a good old-fashioned petition

Gathering names on a petition was once a time-consuming and arduous task, but the Internet has revolutionized the process. Petitions are an easy way for people to show their support and put their name to a cause without too much commitment, and they can also be a catalyst for getting people in power to pay attention.

In 2011 a new website (petitions.whitehouse.gov) was launched by President Obama called We The People, which allows anyone to petition the President directly. If 100,000 people sign up to a petition in its first 30 days, the White House says it will provide a formal response.

There are plenty of other sites that allow anyone to build a petition, including avaaz.org and change.org. If the government isn't your target, these may be a better bet.

There's nothing like face-to-face contact to get people engaged, so if you're campaigning on a local issue it's well worth hitting the streets with pen and paper, too.

Make sure you're addressing the petition to the relevant body, company, or decision-maker. Keep the demands clear, add context to help people digest the issue, and make them aware of how their data will be used. When you've reached your target number, petition hand-ins are also an effective way of getting media attention around your campaign (see Chapter 3).

Some states have mechanisms for propositions, initiatives, and referenda. These allow residents, if they garner enough support, to put questions to the electorate directly, which if passed could change the law. This process will differ on a state by state basis, so speak to a local representative if you need guidance.

AND REMEMBER ...

DON'T BE INTIMIDATED BY

POV

Changing our communities for the better isn't easy. Sometimes it might feel like doors are being slammed and routes are being blocked in every direction, but remember that you must remain persistent. Minds, laws, and lives only change when we refuse to be worn down.

THE PRO-CHOICE ACTIVISTS CHANGING MINDS AT THE HIGHEST LEVEL

In June 2017, the British government announced a u-turn on a policy that forced women from Northern Ireland to pay privately for abortions in the UK—a procedure still criminalized at home. But this change didn't happen overnight. It was triggered by a group of activists who worked closely with MPs, using their passion and knowledge to target those in power.

When Sarah Fox turned up at the inaugural meeting of the London Irish Abortion Rights Campaign in November 2016, she did so with few expectations. "I was looking for a way I could support the struggle for reproductive rights back in Ireland," she recalls twelve months later, "but it had never been obvious to me how to do that before."

The Abortion Act of 1967 partially decriminalized terminations in parts of the United Kingdom, but the law change was never extended to Northern Ireland. "Currently the laws around abortion in Northern Ireland come under a piece of legislation from 1861," explains Sarah. "If convicted you can receive a life sentence in prison. It's absurd."

Angered and frustrated by these outdated laws, Sarah joined one hundred others in a hall that night in London. After introductions the crowd split off into groups, and Sarah joined those tasked with lobbying people in power to bring about a change in these draconian laws. "We thrashed out ideas and strategies, trying hard to figure out what we—as Irish people living in London—could do, and who we should lobby here while also supporting groups at home."

The group identified their aim pretty quickly—to ensure free, safe, and legal abortions across the island of Ireland—but what that might mean in practice in regards to Northern Ireland was far from clear. "Many people in mainland Britain don't feel the current abortion laws are fit for purpose either, so working out our demands was tough." Simply demanding an extension of English law to Northern Ireland wasn't an ideal solution. All present agreed parity was a stepping stone, though; access to abortions must be equal across all corners of the United Kingdom. As it stood, people from Northern Ireland had to pay for abortions in England while residents of other countries in Britain could get them free of charge.

A document was quickly compiled listing every member of Parliament. The activists then conducted research on each MP, looking at how they had voted on similar issues in the past. They also searched for opinions expressed in the media as indications of where their elected representatives might stand. "From there we looked to see who in our group lived in constituencies the more supportive MPs represented while figuring out how we might get them and others onside."

Over the following months the campaign sprang into action. Letters were written and meetings held with MPs, alongside ongoing protests and media campaigns. Sarah's local MP, Labour's Stella Creasy, made it her mission to support the movement's objectives, putting her weight behind the campaign while introducing the activists to professional lobbyists for advice. Meanwhile the Conservative Party, after failing to win a majority in the June 2017 general election, was forced to strike up a deal with the Democratic Unionist Party—a party little known outside of Northern Ireland that, Sarah explains, has long supported anti-abortion policies.

"Suddenly Northern Irish politics was thrown into mainstream British media, and with our preparation done we used this to highlight the fact abortions in Northern Ireland were still illegal. That on average two people a day are forced to travel to the mainland and pay for a procedure the rest of us take for granted."

This perfect storm led to success. In June 2017, Stella Creasy proposed a Bill amendment that would allow people from Northern Ireland to access abortions free of charge in the United Kingdom. Thanks to the dedicated campaigning work of Sarah and her fellow activists, MPs on all sides looked set to vote alongside Creasy, leaving the government facing an embarrassing defeat.

Rather than lose a vote, MPs were assured that there was no longer a need for the amendment, as the government had changed its position. The law would be changed to allow people from Northern Ireland to access abortions in England free of charge.

"There was a lot of learning by doing," Sarah recalls. "None of us really had any experience." From the outset, though, Sarah and her fellow campaigners knew they would need to employ a range of tactics in their efforts to convince politicians to take action. "We certainly used a combination of statistics, facts" and figures to back up our arguments," she recalls, "but personal stories were also integral in winning politicians round. We could show the impact on real people."

"What we've all certainly learned is that no single approach can be taken in isolation. We lobbied hard, but passed motions in trade unions and local political party branches, we marched with the St. Patrick's Day Parade and used social media to raise awareness. From our experience that's the best way to approach forcing change in whatever community or industry you're working in."

ORGANIZE

Come together, stay together,
and build a force for change

INTRODUCTION
—

Activism isn't just about the photo ops
and placards: it's about hard graft behind
the scenes. For every action you pull off,
for every change you make, there'll be
a raft of planning meetings, debates,
and discussions, moments of reflection,
celebrations, and defeats. Laying the
foundations of a movement takes hard work,
but you'll soon find a community that will be
there to support both you and your cause
for the long haul.

Time to assemble

Holding meetings is a great way of growing your activist network, bringing together those already engaged and inviting new people into the fold. If you're just starting out, call your gathering an "open meeting" and encourage anyone who might be interested in getting involved to attend—regardless of what sort of commitment they can make.

As your campaign develops you'll want to hold some closed meetings with just people you know and trust, but maintaining regular open meetings will ensure your network grows.

Scout out a location that is accessible to everyone. Picking a bar, for example, might prevent young people or nondrinkers from attending. Make sure there's wheelchair access and public transport links if possible, too.

One way of ensuring meetings are democratic yet efficient is to share an agenda in advance and ask people to make suggestions. **Once you have an agenda, stick to it. Make sure to keep to time.**

Appointing someone to chair each meeting will help things run smoothly—they'll get you through the agenda and make sure everyone gets their say. Change up who chairs meetings regularly, though, and make sure to keep the position diverse.

FYI

Remember—anyone can attend an open meeting, so if you have sensitive plans or information you don't want the world to know, consider keeping them under wraps.

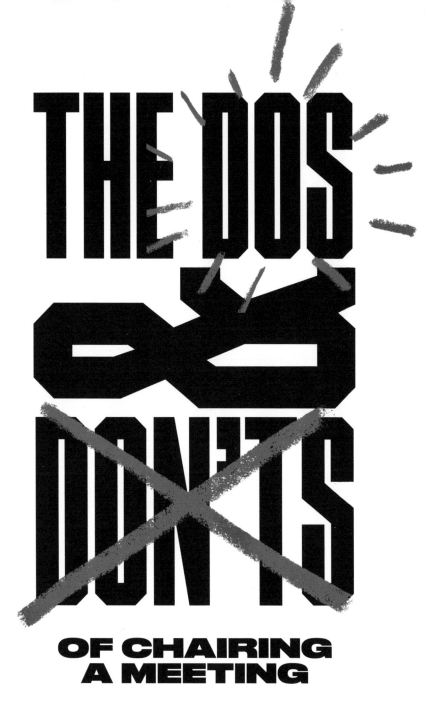

THE DOS & DON'TS OF CHAIRING A MEETING

Arrive early. Give yourself time to prepare.

Start with introductions:
ask everyone to say who they are.

Run through the agenda and
then make sure to stick to it.

Keep your interventions short and sweet—
don't abuse the position.

Don't chair a meeting if you
know you have a lot to say.

Be courteous and respectful of
all opinions (within reason).

If someone is rambling, then move on swiftly.

Keep track of the time.

Everyone deserves to have their voice heard,
so make sure to call on different people.

If people are getting restless, don't
be afraid to call for a break.

Make sure someone is taking
notes and minutes.

Get hands-on

Hand signals in meetings, developed by the Occupy Movement in New York in 2011, are a great way of increasing accessibility while making the consensus decision-making process smoother. By using them, anyone can share their feelings with the chair without a discussion descending into a shouting match.

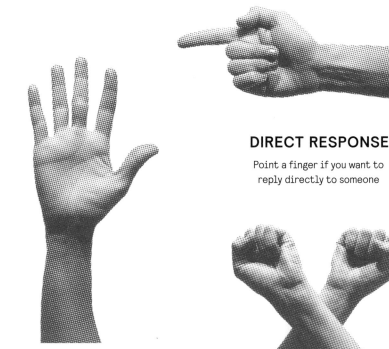

DIRECT RESPONSE

Point a finger if you want to reply directly to someone

WANT TO TALK

Raise one hand in the air if you have a new point to make

BLOCK

When using consensus decision-making, this means "no" to a proposal

POINT OF ORDER

Use this if there's an urgent logistical issue to be raised

OPPOSE

Raise a fist if you want to show serious opposition

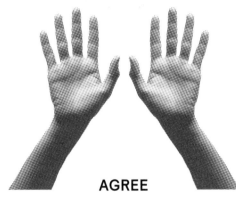

AGREE

Wave your hands in the air to show support for what is being said

CLARIFY

Make this shape with your hand if you don't understand

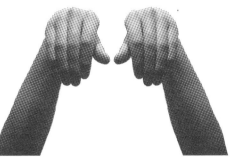

DISAGREE

Drop your hands down if you disagree with a speaker

JARGON BUSTER

SAFE(R) SPACES

Consider drawing up a safe-space (or safer-space) policy to underpin your meetings and wider movement. Write a policy as a group that outlines what behavior is acceptable, and ensure that newcomers are made aware of it. This will help with inclusivity and reduce the risk of prejudice and violence.

INTERSECTIONALITY

Racism, sexism, homophobia, and other forms of discrimination affect people with different identities in different ways, but most forms of oppression are interconnected. This is the basis of intersectionality. Taking account of this in your activism will help ensure that everyone feels included and that your campaign is a space for all.

WORKING GROUPS

By creating working groups dedicated to specific elements
of your campaigning activity, you can help spread the
workload while encouraging people to use and develop their
own expertise. These groups can meet separately from the
main campaign meetings before feeding back and asking
for guidance. They're a great way for new campaigners to
understand the variety of work that needs to be done.

CONSENSUS DECISION-MAKING

Not everyone will agree on everything, but finding a creative
and dynamic way of reaching agreement between all members
of a group is paramount. Instead of majority rule, consensus is
all about being committed to finding solutions that everyone
actively supports, or at least can live with.

Spread the load

When allocating jobs during a meeting, remember that every role is important. Volunteering to stack the chairs away before you go home is as valuable as doing an interview on TV. Play to your strengths and share responsibility, but **don't hold out for the glory.**

One way of ensuring continuity and sharing responsibility is to create subgroups within your network—a fluid collection of people who take responsibility for different aspects of your work. Maybe you want a team to handle **logistics** for meetings, another to oversee **outreach**, and one more to plan an **action**. In between general meetings these groups can get on with the groundwork. They can then report back with updates and provide wider input.

And remember, there's nothing wrong with having fun. Make your meetings as enjoyable as possible, socialize afterward and don't forget to smile.

FYI
—

Ensure that there is a gender balance between those who do more menial work and those who take care of more exciting activities. All too often, women are expected to undertake supporting tasks.

"ALONE WE CAN DO SO LITTLE, TOGETHER WE CAN DO SO MUCH."

Helen Keller,
author and activist

TO DISAGREE

Coming together for a common cause is all well and good, but it's OK not to see eye to eye on everything. Activists or not, we're all on a journey, and the paths that lie ahead can be rocky, with sharp turns and obstacles. Rather than calling out anyone who disagrees with you and taking a high-and-mighty approach, bring people with you by genuinely listening and talking through ideas. To change the world you'll need to change minds.

If rifts start to form between individuals that make cooperation seem impossible, try asking another member of the group—or someone external—to mediate so that issues can be discussed logically, and away from the main group.

THE LGBT+ ACTIVISTS STANDING UP FOR MIGRANTS' RIGHTS

Getting a movement off the ground takes guts and vision, but keeping it going—and actually changing lives—is another matter altogether. For LGSMigrants, this learning curve has been steep but incredibly fruitful. Having found a way to work together, they can now get on with the job: tackling the greatest refugee crisis our generation has ever seen.

We all know how it feels to put the world to rights over a couple of drinks, thrashing out society's problems while searching for solutions with friends. That's exactly what Ben Smoke was doing at a house party back in August 2015, but this conversation wasn't forgotten once the hangover set in. Instead it led to the creation of an activist network—Lesbians and Gays Support the Migrants (LGSMigrants)—which has gone on to build bridges between communities and help shift the toxic narrative about migrants in Britain, while also raising money to support grassroots campaigns.

"We were sat up in a room with a few beers at the peak of the 'migrant crisis'", explains Ben. "Refugee camps in Calais were getting a lot of press, far-right commentators were talking about the need for warships to be sent to attack refugees drowning in the sea. David Cameron—then Prime Minister—dehumanized migrants by referring to them as swarms."

The LGBT+ community has a long tradition of activism and solidarity. During the 1980s' miners strike, another group of queer campaigners came together to form the original LGSM: Lesbians and Gays Support the Miners. Ben and his friends felt it was time for those seeking a better life in Britain to be supported in the same way. The key to success for both groups? Getting organized.

After a few preliminary chats between the founders, an open meeting at a local community center was called. "We created a Facebook page, a Twitter account, and an email", recalls Ben. "Suddenly we found there was a huge appetite within the community to get involved." Ben and his fellow activists came up with a plan of action outlining their ideas, to be presented at the meeting, and over 100 interested people showed up to join them. After a brief introduction, the crowd was split into working groups: fundraising, actions, and events. By the end of the evening, plans were drawn up to hold a direct action outside the Home Office in London, as well as fundraising bucket-shakes in the city center. A charter outlining the group's aims and objectives was also agreed.

"We decided moving forward to have open meetings which would be sovereign in making decisions," Ben continues. "People now make suggestions to the group and, if the room is in agreement, then we act upon it."

In practice, this means people can have a say in LGSMigrants' work and direction without having to commit a lot of their time, allowing more voices to be heard. Facilitators lead these assemblies on a rotating basis: as a horizontal movement—one without leaders—it's imperative that responsibilities are shared across the board.

In between these general meetings, the more regular members of the group are in constant communication. They meet frequently to update one another on each working group's progress, and post on social media to their ever-growing audience, responding to speaking requests and press inquiries whenever they can.

Since its foundation, LGSMigrants has gone on to raise thousands of pounds for organizations working directly to support refugees and migrants. Direct actions include glitter-bombing the offices of a private security firm and, in conjunction with other activist groups, preventing a plane carrying refugees and migrants set to be deported from taking off.

Transparency is key to LGSMigrants' approach to organizing, but when it comes to direct actions that are a little riskier, Ben understands that some decisions must be made behind closed doors. "We can't advertise and discuss our spikier activity in public for obvious reasons," he explains. "These actions were conceived and carried out with a very small group of trusted people. That is difficult in terms of democracy, but it's a necessary evil, because these were the actions that created the biggest splash for us and had a huge impact."

For the most part, however, LGSMigrants are remarkably open. They understand that as important as it is to take action and raise funds, it's also vital that they bring people into their movement—creating a wider network of campaigners while also challenging prejudice and changing minds.

"The connections and relationships LGSMigrants has built within our own group and with other communities is founded in solidarity," Ben reflects, "a term that is an expression of shared struggle, mutual understanding, and respect. For as long as there is sexism, racism, homophobia, and all manner of oppression, LGSM will continue to organize and fight against it."

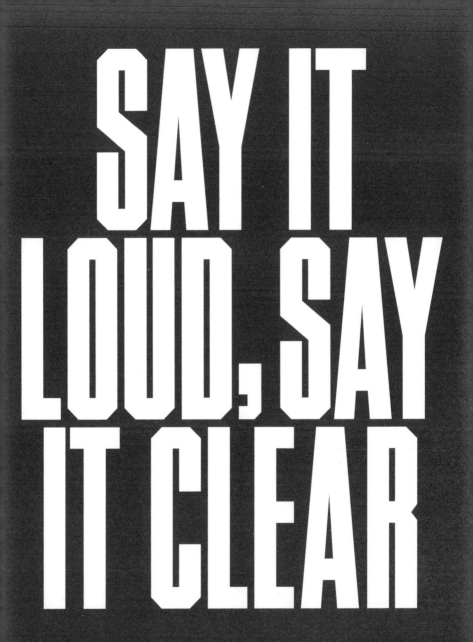

SAY IT LOUD, SAY IT CLEAR

Frame your message, get it out there, and make some noise

INTRODUCTION
—

Building a movement is all about communication, from spreading information among your community to ensuring your message is heard across the world. The Internet has transformed the media landscape for activists, making it easier to reach an audience than ever before, whether by harnessing the power of social media or by directly contacting journalists. You just need to know what it takes to hit the headlines, and how to speak to the people who can get behind your cause.

Hitting the headlines

From local blogs to international newspapers, the work of activists (and yes, it's work) can make the front page. Journalists are always on the prowl for a scoop, and with just a little preparation and coordination, it's easier than you'd think to get your story in the press.

Your first step is to scope out exactly which element of your campaign you want to be picked up, and when. A media strategy should ensure that your story builds and develops for ongoing coverage and attention. Don't let your efforts be reduced to a flash in the pan.

Draw up a timeline of stories you'd ideally see covered: for example, the launch of your movement, the demands from a meeting, the buildup to a protest, and then the victory when you win. Of course you will need to keep this fluid as your plans evolve and grow.

Identifying journalists, commentators, and outlets that'll be interested in your story is vital; sending a universal press release to every staff member at *The New York Times* is far from the best way to ensure your story gets picked up.

Regional media outlets are prime territory for campaigns that affect your local community, but that doesn't mean you shouldn't also hit up the national press. Rolling news channels have plenty of time to fill, too, so don't assume they won't be interested.

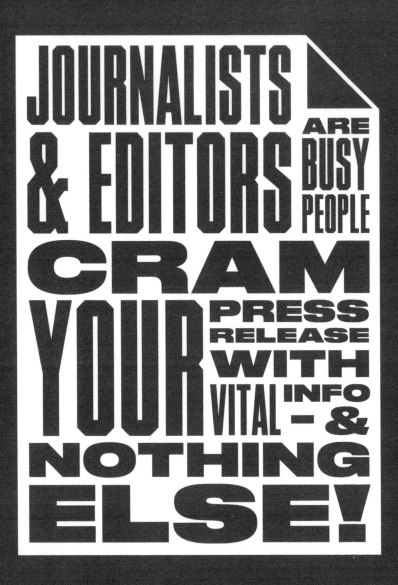

Get the media on board

Drawing up a press release to brief reporters is a simple but often neglected task. Editors and journalists receive hundreds of e-mails every day, so making yours digestible and attention grabbing will help you stand out from the crowd. Keep it concise—no more than a single side of paper, or a couple of paragraphs via e-mail.

Don't be afraid to tweak your release or shift the angle to suit the journalist or outlet you're contacting. Send personalized e-mails where possible: explain why your story is relevant to their readers.

Make sure to include photographs and other relevant visual material whenever contacting journalists. This will help reduce their workload while also ensuring that any reports are as hard hitting as they can be.

Some reporters will want to do the groundwork themselves, but dropping in quotes from activists and experts can lighten their workload. Add contact details at the end so that reporters can get in touch.

Scour the Web and jot down every relevant journalist's contact details. Save their e-mail addresses in a spreadsheet and compile a media list that you can add to and revisit time and time again. Just make sure you never blast out a mass e-mail copying everyone in.

The perfect press release in 6 steps

WHO

Who is involved? Briefly outline who is behind the action.

WHAT

What is happening? Be specific. What news item from your media strategy are you talking about right now?

WHERE

Is there an event, a meeting, or an action that you're pegging the release to? Give as many details as you can, but keep anything confidential under wraps.

WHEN

You can set embargoes if you don't want the story reported immediately; make sure you outline timings of when plans will kick off.

WHY

Set your action or campaign within a broader context. Pull in stats and relate it to other stories to ensure that anyone reading it understands the urgency of what's going on.

HOW

How did this come about? Outline the history of your group, campaign, or movement. Explain your goals and your plans to bring them about.

PRESS RELEASE

SAVE OUR SKATEPARK

Hello Dominique, I hope you're well. My name is Florence and I'm e-mailing you from the campaign group Save Our Skatepark to let you know about a direct action taking place next week which I think will be of interest. On 7 April one hundred skateboarders will be riding through the city centre before holding a "die-in" outside the city hall.

Save Our Skatepark have been protesting plans to demolish the only skatepark in our area. We are a group of...

At 12:30 on Tuesday 7 April, one hundred local skateboarders will meet outside...

Later in the afternoon of 7 April, the committee responsible for deciding the future of the skatepark will be meeting at the city hall. At this meeting, they will...

Given the sensitive nature of the action, please note all stories are embargoed until 7 April at 13:00...

Across the country, skateparks and other public spaces for young people have been forced to close or have faced demolition, as....

For context, in October last year our group formed after proposals were brought forward by...

I really hope you are able to cover this story. We will have a photographer with us on the day and can provide images if necessary.

For further information, please contact us on...
Many thanks, Florence

SEND

Do your homework

Reporters, commentators, and editors will have their own specialisms. Twitter is a great resource for finding out what journalists may be interested in. Research who is writing about the field you're campaigning in and reach out for advice and support. Journalists with a regular platform, such as a weekly column, might pick up the story and run with it. Publications also sometimes throw their weight behind a campaign, so it's worth asking if editors will get on board.

News stories and features about your activism will be written by professionals, but opinion pieces (sometimes called "comment" or "op-eds") are a chance for you to speak on your own terms. Setting up a blog can be a powerful way of self-publishing, but contacting the opinion editors with a pitch in your own words is also well worth a shot. Unlike news reporting, opinion pieces can make a specific argument.

Just remember: campaigns and causes shouldn't be about just one individual. Championing a range of diverse voices will demonstrate that you have a wide base of support.

BUILD

A BUZZ AROUND YOUR STORY AND GIVE IT ROOM TO

GROW

Pitching 101:
the op-ed

Unlike hard news stories, which present the facts and report on what's happening now, comment pieces allow you to make your case in an informed and impassioned way. This is a space where you can be subjective and put forward your opinions in the local and national press. Your voice could be heard by thousands, so it's vital to get your pitch right. Here's how:

- Identify the editor who handles opinion and comment, and make sure you get their name and publication right in your e-mail.
- Don't just copy and paste blanket messages. Tailor your pitch to the publication's area of interest.
- Introduce yourself and make it clear you are pitching an op-ed.
- Explain why you're writing and why you're the best person to speak on this issue.
- Outline your argument briefly and suggest a structure.
- Make it clear you're willing to collaborate and take advice.
- Be realistic about the time you'll need to write it.
- Never send a finished article initially.

JARGON BUSTER

EXCLUSIVE

By offering a story as an exclusive, you guarantee a reporter
or publication first dibs. If you have information that isn't yet
public, it might be worth offering it to one outlet alone. Having
"exclusive" in a headline can generate a buzz and might see your
story given more space and resources, although other outlets
might then be slower to pick up the news afterward.

EMBARGO

If you want to generate some hype or keep information
confidential ahead of an action, then put an embargo on
stories being published—tell outlets that they can't publish
until a given date and time. If multiple pieces are released
in unison, it can help create a storm.

Get your cause the 15 minutes it deserves

Producers on broadcast media (TV and radio) are always on the hunt for interesting guests, and being invited into a studio to make your case can see you reaching millions.

Always ask what format a slot will take—whether it will be an interview, a debate, or a prerecorded segment. If you're going head to head with someone who holds opposing views, be sure to ask for their name and then do some research so that you arrive armed and prepared.

Practice really can make perfect when it comes to TV and radio, so ask someone to help you prepare by firing off questions and getting your soundbites lined up. There are organizations, like labor unions, that offer media training and can help skill-up your network. For starters, these tips may also help:

Dress for the occasion: There's no harm in looking sharp on television. It's important to be comfortable, but don't forget that you're representing a cause.

Bridge your answers: You can't dictate what questions a presenter might ask you, but there are ways of moving a conversation on. Phrases like these will be your best friends: "It would be easy to simply focus on that, but ..." or, "What matters more in this situation is ..." They allow you to offer a response, without detracting from the point you really want to make.

Watch your words: TV and radio is all about spreading your message. Avoid using inflammatory language. Don't overcomplicate the issues either, and steer clear of complex jargon at all costs.

A word of warning

Make sure that you're in control of the narrative when your campaign is spoken about in public. There are certain phrases that might well be used against you by the media or by people opposed to your cause. "Violent" and "anti-democratic" are descriptions used unfairly time and time again to undermine or attack legitimate protests.

FYI

Getting well-known faces to support your campaign will help you gather momentum. Celebrities come with their own audiences, but they can also act as a mouthpiece in the media for your cause. Don't be afraid to reach out, no matter how famous they may be.

"VIOLENCE"

Following protests and actions, the word "violence" can often be thrown around, especially by those looking to demonize and detract from a campaign. Remember, peaceful protest, civil disobedience, and even damage to property do not necessarily equate to violence, so don't be afraid to call people out when they use this word against you.

"ANTI-DEMOCRATIC"

Some critics might label your movement "anti-democratic," especially if you're taking on elected officials or the government at large. Respond to accusations by stating that the right to protest is at the heart of any democracy. Activism is no more or less valid a means for engaging than going to the polls every four years.

Social media (and how to own it)

Social media has changed the game for activists. At the click of a button, it's now possible to reach millions of people on your own terms, and to get your message out there.

Avoid using personal accounts—set up a campaign page on Facebook and other social media platforms so that your audience and network can grow independently from you.

It's also worth having a group of people overseeing each account. Your followers will want to be in touch and comments might need moderating, so spread the workload to make sure you remain on the ball. And if the police start to keep tabs on your campaigning, administrators of your groups or pages might be singled out as ringleaders. The more of you listed, the harder they will find this to do.

Agree on a process for posting to avoid any repetition, confusion, or arguments about tone or message farther down the line.

Be careful what you share, retweet, or endorse: connecting with and supporting other causes can be a great way of building solidarity, but make sure you keep posts focused and aligned with your own group's beliefs.

Find your voice

As we scroll through our newsfeeds, we're increasingly drawn to posts with bite and accounts with a voice. Posting relevant links and updates about your campaign is vital, but starting conversations and grabbing attention will also help your message spread.

To achieve this, you might want to adopt a conversational tone, or be bold and make calls for action. Either way, post regularly to keep your followers in the loop—just try not to "bleed the feed" with incessant posts. You can preschedule posts on Facebook pages, or by using apps like Tweetdeck for Twitter, so you needn't be stuck in front of a screen 24/7. Experiment with posting at different times of the day, too, to see when you get the most engagement.

Social media platforms like Facebook and Twitter are increasingly prioritizing videos, so creating short films with creative allies is another great way of spreading the word.

As awareness is an integral part of growing a movement, you might want to pay to boost your posts. Sponsored posts on Facebook and Twitter allow you to target specific demographics beyond your followers. Targeting those with relevant interests might come at a price, but sometimes it's worth the cost. Platforms make this very straightforward, so just follow the simple steps online.

How to frame your message

Campaigns that succeed in capturing the attention of the public are those that take people on a journey. "Framing" is a term used to describe the process of setting the parameters of a campaign and the change you want to make, and then transmitting this to those who will listen.

You might want a positive frame, such as: "Walk or cycle instead of driving, and we can slow down global warming."

Or you might opt for a negative frame: "If you don't cut down on driving, climate change will spiral out of control."

Keep track of which messages and frames on your social media are shared and engaged with the most, then use these as building blocks to develop and grow.

There are millions of voices shouting loudly on the Internet, but these simple rules will keep your social media campaign focused and on point.

SOCIAL MEDIA TOOLKIT

Hone in on the critical importance of your cause.

—

Be informative. Provide new information that
people might not be aware of.

—

Articulate the need to take action, and provide
a solution. Offer different ways to get involved
and keep your call to action simple.

—

Consistency is integral: tell your story again
and again as it evolves.

—

Connect with people by being emotionally compelling:
try to make your story relatable.

—

Think about what will matter to your audience; frames
can vary, depending on who you are speaking to.

—

Keep it interesting. Photos are always a good draw.

—

Maintain your integrity at all costs:
don't embellish the facts.

AND REMEMBER ...

KEEP YOUR MESSAGE CLEAR &

There's a lot to think about when it comes to communicating your message, but fundamentally it's honesty and integrity that count above all else. Don't let your voice be drowned out by those who wish to silence you, either. Keep your message focused and consistent.

THE YOUTH MOVEMENTS CHANGING POLITICS THROUGH THE POWER OF VIRAL MESSAGING

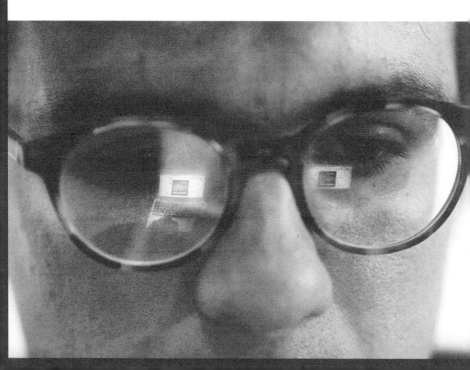

In the United States and Europe, our political systems are becoming increasingly volatile. Fake news and rampant hatred online are spilling over into elections and the mainstream press. But there are ways to cut through the negativity. And it's happening right now, on apps on our phones, thanks to movements such as Momentum that understand the power of "likes."

Placards and petitions are just the tip of the iceberg when it comes to twenty-first-century campaigning; finding new and innovative ways to communicate with and inspire an increasingly diverse public is key. Activists need to compete with the hate-fueled rhetoric that some are intent on peddling, and using social media to do this is a must.

No group in Britain today understands this better than Momentum, a grassroots campaigning network with over 30,000 active members, dedicated to supporting progressive politics. Since Jeremy Corbyn's election as Labour leader in 2015, Momentum has been putting talk of social-movement politics into action. And fundamental to doing this, even in the group's early stages, has been how they connect online.

"Social media allows us to directly communicate with masses of people in a personal way for very little money," explains 25-year-old organizer Joe Todd. "You can talk to people without having to persuade those in positions of power to listen to what you want to say."

Momentum have stats that show their method is working. In the last week of the UK's 2017 general election, nearly one in four UK Facebook users had watched a Momentum video on the site. One of their videos reached more than 6 million views. The mainstream press was hostile to Momentum and its messages, but that didn't prevent them cutting through.

Exactly the same outlook proved instrumental in capturing the imaginations of the millions who got behind Bernie Sanders' presidential campaign. When Sanders announced his candidacy, only 5 percent of Americans had heard of him. Social media helped make him a household name.

"Part of that was through millions of shares of official campaign content," explains Claire Sandberg, his former digital organizing director. "But it was also grassroots content—memes, graphics, videos—created by regular people and circulated with the #FeeltheBern hashtag. People got their own message out, and converted their friends to supporters."

Joe Todd agrees. "If you're a small activist organization, getting traction in the mainstream press is tough: finding contacts, utilizing resources—your story might not be seen as newsworthy. Through social media, that barrier is no longer there. Small campaigns have generated a lot of support recently through creating interesting content placed directly onto social media."

According to Joe, Momentum's video output on social media can generally be split into two distinct categories: content aimed at mobilizing their core supporters, and content they hope will go viral, reaching whoever it can.

"These types of videos are different," Joe explains. "One might never reach millions of views because you're speaking to a certain section of society—your base, the people who will go out and actually do things you ask of them. For the other, you're just trying to make as big an impact as possible to get people talking. We're reaching people from all sides of the political spectrum with these videos we produce."

If the Momentum team have learned anything from their social media experiences, it's that thinking about who you are trying to speak to, and what you are trying to achieve, is vital. The more innovative ways you can find to do this, reckons Joe, the better.

During the general election, Momentum were miles ahead of other campaign groups—their use of WhatsApp on polling day being just one example of many. "We used WhatsApp to create a viral message," Joe continues. "In short, you'd receive a message from a mate saying something along the lines of: 'Today is election day, vote Labour; if you want to send on this message click this link.'"

"It forwarded you to a website we set up, which then took you back onto WhatsApp with a broadcast message to send to all your contacts. It literally took minutes and soon you'd have communicated directly with as many people as you wanted to."

According to their analysis, well over 400,000 people read that message on voting day, which in one 24-hour period was no mean feat.

"The fact that we've got all these people passionate and enthused by politics is exciting," concludes Joe. "If you can harness properly the technological and social media tools we have available, then the possibilities of who a movement can speak to, and how it speaks to them, are truly endless."

DESIGN YOUR FUTURE

From placards and posters
to symbols and signs

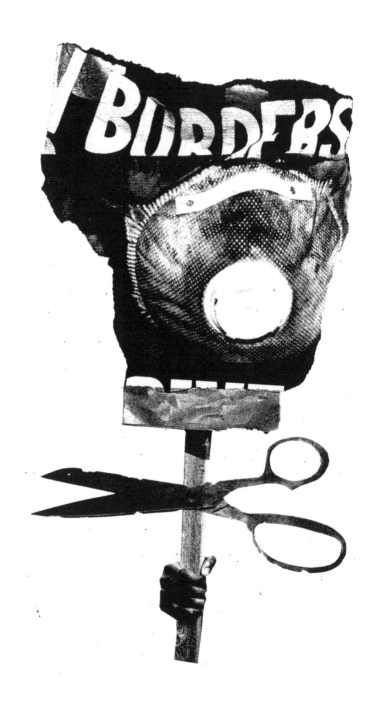

INTRODUCTION
—

Activism is all about making the most of the materials and means we have at our disposal, using what limited resources we may have to make our message as loud and clear as possible. What you may lack in multimillion-dollar budgets and fancy agencies can be made up for with creativity and embracing the activist's favorite acronym: DIY.

Branding isn't just for the big guys

As your campaign expands and evolves, it's worth scoping out ways to build a brand. That doesn't mean corporate jargon and billboard campaigns: good design and clear messaging are all you need to make your mark. A simple slogan on its own might not seem much, but articulating your message in a single, repeated phrase will help ensure that what you have to say is carried far and wide.

Words are important, but so are visuals. An effectively designed logo can be a powerful way to make your movement instantly recognizable, so scout out the skills of those involved in your campaign and wider community, and brainstorm how your broader mission could be represented in a simple drawing.

Another option is to take a color, symbol, or shape and start using it on all your campaign materials—a simple, repeated sign that can be replicated time and time again. In the same way that we all know what a red ribbon signifies when worn around World AIDS day, there's no reason why you can't create a unique emblem that will be inextricably linked to your campaign.

One of the most successful examples of art and activism colliding was the work done by ACT UP, an LGBT+ direct-action and advocacy campaign group. Growing out of New York City in the 1980s, ACT UP set out to improve the lives of people with AIDS. These activists took a pink triangle and the slogan "SILENCE = DEATH," and turned it into an international symbol that resonates across the globe to this day.

SILENCE = DEATH

How to make the perfect placard in 3 steps

The humble placard can be an activist's best friend—
a visual representation of your beliefs for all the world to
witness. Put in the time to make it sturdy, so that neither
your message nor your handiwork are a protest flop.

1 | FIGURE OUT WHAT YOU'RE SAYING

A powerful placard must have an instant impact, so honing in
on your message is a must. Snappy slogans are always welcome,
but humor or emotive messages can work well, too. Keep
the text as brief as possible or people won't have time to
digest your words.

2 | DESIGN YOUR SIGN

Sketch out your slogan on a piece of paper, scoping out how
much space you'll need for words, symbols, and images when
it is scaled up. Remember, you can work with two separate
designs on a double-sided placard, so don't be afraid to
mix it up.

Big, bold text will grab onlookers' attention, so make sure your
words can be seen from afar. Don't be afraid to drop in some
decorations, either—express yourself however you like, as long
as it supports the message.

3 | BUILD, BUILD, BUILD

Pick your materials carefully—the execution matters. If you're
traveling far or the weather looks set to be wild, make sure you
opt for a durable surface. Think poster board, heavy-duty card,
or corrugated plastic. If you're keeping to a strict budget, then
dumpster diving outside stores is a great place to start.

You'll also need a handle to get your placard waving high. Size
up the length you need, and bear in mind that you'll need extra
height on the handle so that it can reach to the very top of your
sign for stability. Plywood, dowel rod, or disused broom handles
are always winners, but make sure you choose something that
will be comfortable to hold for long periods of time.

To build your placard, lay one side facedown on the ground,
then place the handle in the center. Attach the handle to the
sign with glue, tape, staples, or nails—or a combination for extra
security. Position the second poster face up on top, secure it,
and you're done.

FYI
—
There's nothing worse than finding a splinter in your finger
if you're out protesting for a long stretch, so try wrapping
your placard handle in tape or fabric. You'll then be free to
concentrate on marching loud and proud.

Stand out from the crowd

Banners are another effective way of spreading your message—carrying them with you as you march or take action will help keep you visible. Bedsheets and paint are an easy go-to if you're on a budget, but as your campaign matures it might become worth investing in something a little more professional.

Banners can also be the centerpoint of a direct action (see Chapter 7).

The art of the banner drop is incredibly simple: take a boldly printed banner and hang it somewhere—with or without permission. Activists will often target high-profile public spaces: think bridges, shopping malls, the center of a college campus. Secure weights to the bottom of your banners to keep them stable in the wind.

If you don't ask permission, a banner will be taken down, so in order to make an impact, timing is everything: pick your moment carefully. And if you are somewhere you shouldn't be, remember that the police might take action against you (see Chapter 6).

FYI
—
Cut wind holes into any big banners you intend to carry on marches and protests. This will stop you from being swept away down the street.

Time to assemble

If you're coordinating an action, it's worth setting aside time for your fellow activists to come together and get creative with placards, banners, and other props. Holding a making day is a tried-and-tested way of getting people excited before any big event.

Find an accessible and open space—think church halls, community centers or even an outdoor area in the summer—and invite people down on an evening or weekend to get involved. If you've got the budget, then bring along communal materials and encourage anyone attending to bring resources with them, too.

Days like this won't just leave you with attention-grabbing creations, you'll also find it builds excitement and helps a community start to form.

There'll be some people keen to support your cause who might not be able to attend a protest, action, or rally. Holding events like this offers them an alternative way to get involved.

Why not ask those who join you to make extra placards and posters? There's nothing wrong with being overprepared. Provide refreshments and play music through a set of speakers; this will help keep people around and engaged for the day.

Prepare your props

Banners and placards are activist staples, but that doesn't mean there's no space to find other ways to get creative for a cause. Think carefully about whether visuals, props, or objects could complement your actions.

When Greenpeace activists wanted to draw the world's attention to melting polar ice caps, they built a giant polar bear to make people take note. The bear was paraded through the streets at protests around the Paris Climate Talks; it was parked outside Shell's London headquarters when the company intended to continue with damaging plans to drill for oil in the Arctic.

On a smaller scale, you might wish to think simple: inflatables, cardboard cutouts, and flags are just some of the props you could employ. These won't just help in making your action feel cohesive; eye-catching imagery might also find its way onto social media and into the mainstream press.

Costumes are also a failsafe way to get onlookers talking, providing photographers and the media with an image that's sure to generate buzz. Activists from the British women's and nonbinary campaign group Sisters Uncut dressed as suffragettes outside the Houses of Parliament to highlight the need for more provision for survivors of domestic violence. People dressed as dinosaurs marched outside the White House to demonstrate against President Trump's cuts to national service programs like the Peace Corps.

If there's a particular color associated with your campaign, then why not ask those attending an action to come dressed in clothes to match?

Hack the system

We have no say in the corporate messages that we're bombarded with every day. From billboards at the bus stop to adverts on the subway, our eyes and ears are assaulted with information we seldom need.

There's a reason why companies throw endless resources into advertising—whether you like it or not, it works. Luckily, there are ways of getting your message onto giant billboards in order to co-opt this prime real estate for your cause. Employing some guerrilla tactics like ad-hacking might be the order of the day. Just tread carefully with how you go about it. And keep your message short and smart.

FYI
—

You don't need to leave a permanent mark to commit a criminal offence, so think carefully about where and how you use chalk, paints, or pencils to mark property without permission. See Chapter 6 for more.

JARGON BUSTER

AD-HACKING

It might sound like a complex technological process, but the art of ad-hacking is anything but complicated. It simply means reclaiming the advertising space that covers our streets, towns, and cities—replacing the corporate crap with more meaningful messages.

The ad-hacker's starter pack

There's no right or wrong way to ad-hack,
but it's worth bearing a few things in mind.

Stickers can be a fast way to hit and run.
But be warned: this isn't legal. Some activists
cover their faces to avoid being identified.

It might sound obvious, but ads aren't all the same size,
so make sure to do a recce with a tape measure.

Be creative about where you target:
bar restrooms, train carriages, and
noticeboards are all prime spots.

Scope out whether you can place your
ads over the top of what's already in place—
having to take down ads or mess with property
might see you run into trouble with the law.

Printing professionally might give your ads a longer
lifespan—be bold and original with your messaging,
but keep your designs sharp and sleek.

Keep a low profile—ad-hack at the quietest time of the day.

Build hype by sharing your creations on social media.
You'll be surprised at how quickly word can spread.

AND REMEMBER ...

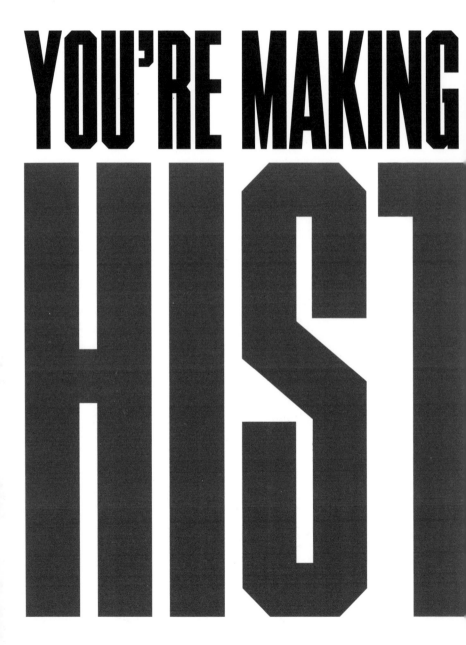

YOU'RE MAKING
HIST

From placards to banners, stencils to badges, the tools activists produce aren't just works of art, they're artifacts of change. Whenever possible, document your creations by taking photographs of them. One day, these could be icons for others to take inspiration and learn from.

THE STORY OF A HUMBLE RED SQUARE THAT BECAME A SYMBOL OF RESISTANCE

Pairing your mission with a striking symbol is a tried-and-tested way of connecting with allies and spreading your message. For student activists in Quebec, a simple red square became an icon that went on to grab a nation's attention.

In 2012, the province of Quebec in eastern Canada bore witness to a student uprising, a wave of strikes, protests, and activism brought about by a government intent on implementing a 75 percent tuition-fee hike over a five-year period. Students refused to attend their lectures, and entire campuses found themselves shut down.

What started out as a response to a specific policy took no time at all to become a whole lot more, as other groups feeling marginalized and forgotten piled on to show their solidarity and broaden the cause.

Student assemblies gathered and made decisions using direct democracy, counterposed against a government that was in the midst of corruption scandals and seemed to the public anything but democratic and fair.

This wave of activism became synonymous with images of police repression, of creative direct actions, of tens of thousands of Quebeckers taking to the streets for months on end to make themselves seen and heard. But no symbol really captured the imagination or spirit of the movement as much as the humble red square.

"It was there from the start; it was always the symbol of the student fight," explains Béatrice Chateauvert-Gagnon over Skype from Montreal, where, back in 2012, she was actively involved in campaigning for the cause. This simple symbol of resistance had first been used in a smaller student revolt in 2005, but it was seven years later that it truly took on a life of its own. Often made of felt and placed on items of clothing, the emblem quickly spread. Student unions handed them out in droves, but being so simple to make, the red square was very much fueled by DIY.

Students and their supporters pinned small red squares to their lapels, while in colleges and across communities, scaled-up squares were placed in windows and storefronts by those proudly looking to display their support. The square became a public display of resistance, an act of subtle yet unapologetically in-your-face defiance, whether worn in Parliament, on television, or when browsing at your local store—your colors quite literally pinned to the mast.

"In 2012 the red square became connected to the expression 'We are in the red'—that, as students, we had no money; our bank accounts were in the red zone. The color red also embodied the deep anger students felt toward the government," explains Béatrice. "Wearing one would start a discussion, it would get people talking; they might challenge you or show their support." Whatever the outcome of a discussion, this little piece of fabric had the ability to start conversations.

It wasn't long before the red square had become so powerful that those who opposed what the activists stood for attempted to create their own symbol—a green square worn by a minority of students who wanted to show their disapproval of the resistance. Students at the University of Sussex in the UK meanwhile followed the lead of their Canadian counterparts and used yellow squares in their own campaigns on campus.

As the protests developed, tensions heightened and the symbol developed beyond the limits of its four edges. "People captured the squares in situ and took photographs that later became exhibitions," recalls Béatrice. "Activists would blockade the metro to cause disruption or hold die-ins dressed entirely in red."

The symbol had become synonymous with the movement, and soon the color red—and therefore the movement—was everywhere.

Today the red square can stir up mixed emotions in Quebec: a bittersweet emblem of the highs and lows that activists went through, which remain with them to this day. "The red square became an international symbol of student resistance, but here it is associated with a moment of history, with nostalgia," suggests Béatrice, "but also a reminder of the battles that were fought, both lost and won." The Quebec government changed, and the planned 75 percent tuition hike was shelved.

"To me, the red square will forever be a symbol of a moment of freedom and disobedience—of a generation politicized and taking to the streets each and every night, putting their bodies on the line together. And who knows? One day it might even come back."

TAKE TO THE STREETS

Grab a placard and get marching

INTRODUCTION
—

While it's true that there's no one-size-fits-all solution to pushing forward with a cause, no single tactic that'll guarantee a win, marches are the lifeblood of activist movements. There's something empowering—almost magical—about taking to the streets in a democracy and reclaiming the public paths that for so long have been ours to march down.

International movements and NGOs sometimes organize massive marches that you can participate in, but the most powerful and spontaneous in recent history have emerged from grassroots campaigns.

From rallies with a handful of people that end in a parade down a quiet side street to protests that see thousands marching on Washington, DC, there's strength to be found in numbers.

Choose your moment carefully

Timing, as always, is key. Weekends might seem an obvious choice, but remember that while potential attendees might not be working, nor will those in power who you want to be taking notice. If you're in the city, early evenings can often work a treat, especially if the issue is urgent. It's also worth checking for major sports games, public holidays, and other events planned in the vicinity to avoid potential supporters having commitments elsewhere. This is all about getting boots on the ground.

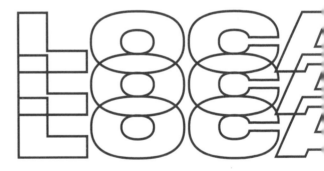

Think carefully about where you want people to gather and find a place for them to assemble before marching from A to B. Make sure that you also find out whether the land you pick is public or private: the First Amendment of the Constitution states that you generally have a right to assemble in public spaces which don't have specific restrictions, but if there's a private owner you can be moved on with no warning at all (see Chapter 6).

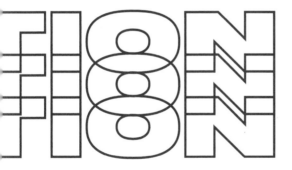

Plot out the route you hope to take, and if you want to be visible, stick to the busiest streets. Protests and marches are supposed to be disruptive, but if you've communicated your plans well in advance, and make your intentions clear on the day, the inconvenience to others will be minor. Do your homework and onlookers will then honk their horns and show their support, instead of getting annoyed.

Get people talking

Once you've picked a place, date, and time, you're ready to make your protest public. Make an event on Facebook, and invite your friends, family, and other supporters of the cause. It's worth managing your expectations, though—not everyone who clicks "going" on a Facebook event will show up on the day.

Partner up with organizations that may have engaged audiences of their own. Draw up a press release (see Chapter 3) and e-mail it to news sites and stations, both local and national.

Local newspapers and regional news sites are always looking for stories, so try to get some coverage in the build-up to the march—it'll help spread the news in advance. Posters and flyers might be old school, but they're still a great way of creating a buzz if you want your march to be a success.

FYI
—

Create a team of reliable people who'll be able to give you a hand (WhatsApp groups are a great way of keeping in contact) and assign everyone specific roles. Make sure to meet before the march kicks off, and hold a debrief afterward.

March must-haves

The endpoint of a march is an exciting climax, an opportunity to regroup and mobilize the community that's turned out to show its support.

You might want to ask people to speak from a podium, and if you do you'll need a way to make sure they are heard. Here's a checklist of the vital considerations for your march.

Invite a range of relevant speakers who'll bring support.
Give them each a time limit and stick to it.

Find someone to act as a host.

Appoint press liaisons to get
the message out there, and police liaisons
to communicate with officers on the day.

Think about access:
is your route wheelchair-friendly?

Invite performers to get the crowd excited
at the start or endpoint of the march.

Create a hashtag if you want your message to trend.

If the route is complex,
draw up maps and hand them out.

Give stewards fluorescent jackets to direct
the crowd and keep an eye on traffic.

Grab a first aid kit, just in case.

Bring a megaphone or microphone—
it's important to be heard.

Whistles or drums? Make some noise.
Chanting is also a great way to fire people up.

Make sure someone is taking photos and video,
and posting online in real time.

Control your visual messages

Chapter 4 covered protest art in all its finest forms, but each march needs to have a strong message. Encouraging attendees to be creative and show up with their own contributions is great, but if there's a slogan, phrase, or image you want repeating, let those invited know in advance. Visual messages are key.

One useful way of guaranteeing that your message gets heard is by plastering it on a road-width banner. This will look great in pictures and provide a clear explanation of what's going down. It will also allow you to keep control of your group and track of how fast people are moving: coming to a halt behind a banner gives everyone time to regroup.

While solidarity and support from other groups is always worth embracing, be careful that your protest isn't co-opted by groups with their own agenda. You may want to ask certain groups not to bring their own branded placards if they are not relevant to your cause and action.

A little bit
of law

Under American law, if you're organizing a public march that isn't restricted to sidewalks, you're obliged to obtain a permit from the relevant authority. In some cases this can take a matter of weeks. This only applies if you're the organizer; if you just plan on attending, or are part of helping make plans, then you don't need to worry.

Sometimes marches are responsive, with less time for planning, in which case you may decide to notify the authorities as soon as possible. Not everyone decides to follow these rules.

The authorities may want to know the date and time of the march, the route you'll be taking, as well as the names and addresses of the march's organizers. They have the power to limit or change the route, and set other conditions on your march known as time, place, and manner restrictions. In some circumstances they'll change the location, limit the number of attendees, or call a halt to a sit-down protest if it blocks road traffic or pavements.

If your protest will be static then you are not obliged to obtain a permit.

FYI

Legal observers are trained volunteers who support the legal rights of activists. They provide basic legal guidance and act as independent witnesses of police behavior at protests. Appoint trained people and put them in high-vis jackets. They will be your eyes and ears on the ground should anything not go to plan. Activist networks in your area may run training sessions if you wish to become a legal observer. Otherwise contact the National Lawyers Guild. (See Chapter 6 for more legal advice.)

AND REMEMBER ...

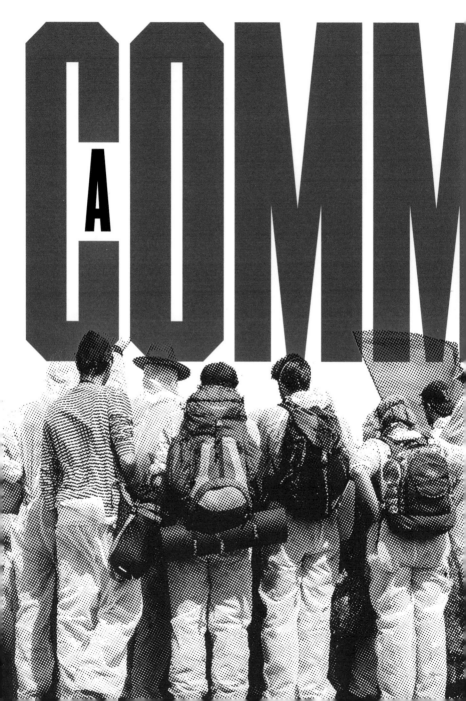

UNITY IS IN THE MAKING

Marches and rallies aren't just a show of force, but a chance to feel powerful, meet like-minded people and create a network that lasts. Don't let the momentum dissipate. For example, you might decide to hold another rally after the march is over. Ask stewards to take names and contact details to keep people in the loop about future plans, and maybe have a social afterward.

HOW THE WOMEN'S MARCH ON WASHINGTON WENT GLOBAL

On a sunny Saturday in January 2017, one of the largest globally synchronized protests in history took place in over 600 locations worldwide, in resistance to a rising tide of racist and sexist rhetoric fueled by Donald Trump's election as US President. It all started with a single message on Facebook and a group of first-timers demanding to be heard.

On 8 November 2016, as the US election results rolled in red state after red state, frustrated people across the globe sat down at their computers and searched for solace. They were connecting with like-minded people, motivated to organize against the sexist and bigoted values being espoused by the newly elected Donald Trump and his supporters. Trump called women ugly and said abortions should be "punishable." A leaked recording also revealed the future President boasting about grabbing women by the "pussy." Disenfranchised women were looking for outlets for their anger—rallies they could attend in order to show their disapproval of the new administration.

New York-based chef Breanne Butler was one of these people. When she logged on to Facebook the night after the election, she saw a post by a friend of a friend named Bob Bland about organizing a march on Washington, DC for the day after Trump's inauguration on 21 January. Breanne messaged Bob: "How can I help?" Bob messaged her back instantly: we need you to make Facebook pages for a march in every state of America.

"When I got involved there were just a couple thousand people confirmed to attend," explains Breanne, "but by that weekend the number was up to six figures. Then it just kept rising. I thought it was going to break Facebook." More and more people began volunteering, too. Breanne recalls, "We didn't have time to stop and ask questions or do background checks on people; it was like: 'Are you breathing? Great. Wanna volunteer?' It was just regular people stepping up to the plate."

The march, which by this point had evolved from the "Million Woman March" (a name already taken by a race-related march that had been held in 1995) to "Women's March on Washington," soon found itself with sister events far beyond US borders. Within 24 hours of getting involved, Breanne was answering e-mails from strangers reaching out to organize a Women's March on London, a Women's March on Toronto, and similar events in Geneva and Oslo.

In Rome, a US foreign national called Elizabeth Farren had come across the Washington March in "post-election despair," and reached out to a woman she'd met at the Democrats Abroad election-night party in the hope of organizing a rally for US expats in Italy. In Melbourne, an American teacher named Melissa Goffin considered buying flights home to the US for the Washington march, but finding them too expensive decided to set up a march of her own in Australia.

In Kenya, an expat, employee of Human Rights Watch, and mother of two, Neela Ghoshal, joined a group called "Progressive Americans in Kenya," for American women who were angry about the election result and didn't want to "sit siloed in Nairobi." They set up a rally, too. Meanwhile, in Stockholm, Lotta Kuylenstierna read about the Washington march, then went ahead and made a Facebook page of her own. She had already called the police for a permit when she contacted the US organizers.

These marches created a platform for radical thinking, but they were also about different groups coming together and learning from one another. At the marches, attended by millions around the globe, women, men, and children from all backgrounds stood united on the street—or in Kenya's case, in a forest.

These shows of solidarity are a shining example of how marches can flick a switch inside so many. What started as a feeling of disenfranchisement and hopelessness turned into a powerful display of strength, just because a handful of people decided to stand up and be counted.

KNOW YOUR RIGHTS

Be ready for every eventuality

INTRODUCTION
—

Organizing collectively and taking action as a movement can be a life-changing experience. It will give you a sense of empowerment and hope that enters your bloodstream and will run through your veins for a long time to come. Change, however, isn't always welcomed by those in charge. If you encounter repression and violence, you won't just be left with physical scars; make a wrong move and your newfound strength will be ripped from your hands. That's why it's crucial to be prepared and know your legal rights.

Our rights
are everything

The Bill of Rights (the first ten amendments to the US
Constitution) enshrined our right to protest in law, and people
in the United States have, throughout its history, stood up
for these freedoms. Supreme Court cases, such as Texas v.
Johnson have since further cemented our right to free speech
and assembly, although over time the state has introduced
laws and regulations to restrict us. That said, if you understand
your rights and know where to find support, exercising these
freedoms can be easy.

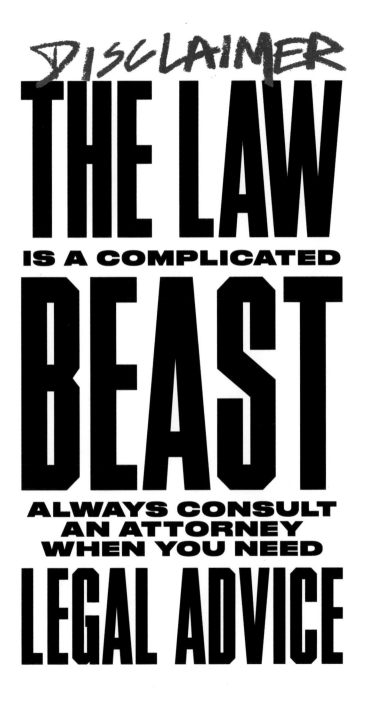

Understand the lay of the land

When it comes to where your right to protest can be exercised, knowing who owns the land you stand on is essential. Most land owned by the government, including public highways, should be accessible for protests and marches. If the element of surprise is not important, it might be worth speaking to the authorities in charge beforehand, just in case there are local ordinances or procedures you are required to follow that may restrict your access. In practice, though, public land is normally ours to meet on. It's not always obvious if land is privately owned.

Think of this as someone else's back garden: we have few rights to protest on land owned by corporations or individuals, so if you're looking to hold a rally or a march from A to B, make sure you find out who owns what by contacting your local city hall or municipal center.

Laws at both state and federal levels make it an offense to damage or destroy someone else's property, so think carefully before partaking in any activity that leads to this as a result. Some courts have found that using chalk to draw on a sidewalk, even while water-soluble, can be considered an offense. Maximum punishments depend on the severity of the damage.

To trespass or not to trespass?

A superstore gives you permission to walk down their aisles to grab your groceries, but that doesn't give you license under the law to do whatever you want while inside. However, taking action on private land might be the tactic you opt for, especially if you're targeting a corporation and you want your campaign to be seen. A landowner can quickly withdraw permission granted to you to be on their land—and if they do, you will be trespassing. For example, a superstore manager could ask you to leave if you were to stage a protest in their store. Although trespass is not always a criminal offence, landowners have a right to forcibly remove trespassers and, in some cases, demand damages in court.

Generally, though, should you refuse to leave when asked, they will just call the police. If you fail to comply with an officer's orders, you may then be arrested.

FYI
—

Activists have long used occupations as a tactic for reclaiming space, grabbing attention and creating a base for their cause. Legally speaking, these are a whole different ball game, so do your homework and check out the reading list in this book before setting up camp.

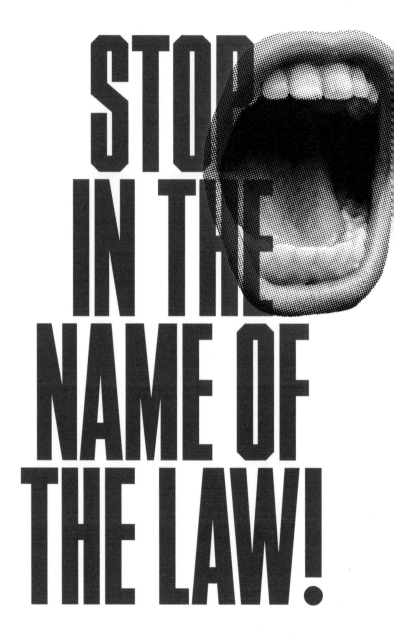

Stop and identify

In certain jurisdictions, there is a statutory power authorizing police to stop someone and legally obtain their identification without needing to have reasonable suspicion of a crime having been committed. Even in "stop and identify" states, there is no legal obligation for the person that has been stopped to provide identification if there is no reasonable suspicion of a crime having been committed.

If the police officer does have reasonable suspicion, and the state has "stop and identify" laws, it is an offense not to identify yourself. The suspicion of a crime having been committed, or about to be committed, must be reasonable and clearly articulable.

At any time a police officer may approach someone on the street and question them, even if there are not grounds for detention or arrest. Often this is with the intention of getting enough information to formulate the reasonable suspicion element of a detention or arrest. A police officer is often not required to notify the person stopped that they don't have to answer any questions, but this can be ascertained by asking, "Am I free to go?" If the answer is affirmative, you are within your rights to leave.

Make sure to ascertain the legal situation in your state.

Stop and frisk

Also known as a Terry Frisk, a name derived from a US Supreme
Court case, "Terry" rules allow an officer to briefly detain you if
they have reasonable and clearly articulable grounds to suspect
you have engaged in, or are about to engage in, criminal activity.
These grounds need to be "reasonable" on the basis of a
"reasonable police officer", and determined on the "totality"
of the facts.

If you are stopped for a Terry frisk, an officer may conduct
a "pat down" of your outer garments and confiscate any
contraband in line with the "plain view doctrine." This means an
officer may confiscate any contraband, but only if its presence
is immediately apparent.

Keep your cool

If you are stopped and searched under any of these powers, get someone else to record your interaction with the police, if possible. The American Civil Liberties Union (ACLU) provides the following advice to follow if you are stopped for questioning by an officer:

Stay calm. Don't run. Don't argue, resist, or obstruct the police, even if you are innocent or the police are violating your rights. Keep your hands where police can see them.

Ask if you are free to leave. If the officer says yes, calmly and silently walk away. If you are under arrest, you have a right to know why.

You have the right to remain silent and cannot be punished for refusing to answer questions. If you wish to remain silent, tell the officer out loud. In some states, you must give your name if asked to identify yourself.

You do not have to consent to a search of yourself or your belongings, but police may "pat down" your clothing if they suspect a weapon. You should not physically resist, but you have the right to refuse consent for any further search. If you do consent, it can affect you later in court.

Face coverings

For many reasons, activists will sometimes wish to hide their identity. The Constitution guarantees the right to wear masks and face coverings as a "symbolic form of speech" under the First Amendment. In recent years, some states have attempted to restrict the right of protesters to wear face coverings. One such example can be seen in North Dakota, as a response to the Dakota Access Pipeline protests. Such laws are yet to be challenged at the Supreme Court.

Legal helplines

It's impossible to predict whether the police will use their powers at a protest, so preparing yourself and your fellow activists is vital. Create a legal helpline on the day of any action, so that you can keep track of police actions and arrests. Buy a new pay-as-you-go SIM and put it into a phone. Ask someone behind the scenes to monitor it and make notes during a march or action, as witnesses might call in to report incidents on the ground. Make sure this phone number is circulated around. These reports will provide a valuable resource should cases end up in court.

Miranda Rights

In 1966, the US Supreme Court decided the historic case of Miranda v. Arizona. In this ruling, it was declared that whenever a person is taken into police custody, he or she must be explicitly told about their Fifth Amendment right not to make any self-incriminating statements.

As a result of this case, anyone in police custody must be told four things before being questioned:

1 | You have the right to remain silent.

2 | Anything you say can and will be used against you in a court of law.

3 | You have the right to an attorney.

4 | If you cannot afford an attorney, one will be appointed for you.

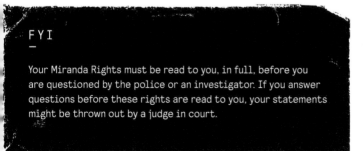

FYI
—

Your Miranda Rights must be read to you, in full, before you are questioned by the police or an investigator. If you answer questions before these rights are read to you, your statements might be thrown out by a judge in court.

Crowd control

Kettling, or containment, is a technique used by the police to bring large crowds under their control. Kettles can be imposed for long periods of time, so if you're heading to a protest where a kettle might occur, take water, supplies, warm clothes, and your phone.

Some states have laws which allow for protesters to be arrested en masse if they refuse to comply with orders to disperse. If you are ordered to disperse but believe the order may be unlawful, you may be able to challenge the legality of the order at a later date.

JARGON BUSTER

KETTLE

Sometimes referred to as a kettle, containment
is a tactic employed by the police to seal off
protesters in a given space for a period of time,
if they believe it is necessary to prevent disorder
or protect public safety.

Facing arrest

Facing arrest is stressful and unpleasant, even if you know you're having your liberty taken away for a cause. In some situations, activists engage in civil disobedience with the expectation of being put in handcuffs. At other times, the police might arrest you before you've even had a chance to pause for thought.

The National Lawyers Guild (NLG) is a grassroots network of lawyers who support people facing legal action for their involvement in protest, and it's worth consulting their advice pages and local chapters for state-specific information.

Here are five tips worth remembering should you find yourself facing arrest, in line with advice from the NLG:

1 | Remain silent—The Fifth Amendment of the Constitution provides you with the right to remain silent. Tell an officer you wish to do this, and seek an attorney immediately. Don't say anything, sign anything, or make any decisions without an attorney.

2 | Personal details—In some states you can be detained or arrested for merely refusing to give your name under 'stop and identify' statutes, if officers have reasonable suspicion that you may have committed a crime. Providing a false name could in some circumstances be a crime.

3 | Find a good attorney—Identify which legal firms in your area, or in the vicinity of the protest, specialize in protest and activism cases. Write their phone number on your arm in case you are arrested, as your belongings may be confiscated. When you are offered the right to legal representation, call them.

4 | What power?—The police often rely on activists not knowing the law or their rights. Always ask under what powers officers are asking you to do something; likewise if they arrest you. The police have a duty to keep you informed. Make a note of who they are and what they say as soon as possible.

5 | Under 18—If you're a minor, you also have the right to remain silent. You cannot be arrested for refusing to talk to the police, although in some states you may have to give your name if you have been detained. If you're detained in a juvenile hall following arrest, normally you must be released to a parent or guardian.

Hold the police to account

Sometimes officers will act wrongly, but even the police aren't above the law of the land. Legal procedures can be tricky to navigate, so if you feel you've been treated unfairly, consult a attorney with experience to look into your case.

You may be able to make a claim against the police if you've been assaulted or mistreated, wrongly arrested, or prosecuted for something you didn't do. Your attorney will be best placed to advise you. This could result in an apology, damages being awarded, or an admission of wrongdoing by the police.

As soon as possible, note down every detail you remember from the incident, including officers' patrol car and badge numbers, which agency the officers were from, and any other details.

Get contact information for any witnesses. Take photographs of any injuries you have incurred.

With this information, you will be able to file a written complaint with the agency's internal affairs division or civilian complaint board. In some cases, you may be able to file a complaint anonymously. This may also result in you taking the police to court.

PREPARE FOR ALL EVENTU

Staying on the right side of unjust laws isn't always easy, and even if you do, there is no guarantee you won't end up intimidated, arrested, or under attack. Keeping yourself informed of your legal rights is the best way to ensure you're ready for whatever is thrown at you. Whatever happens, though, remember to stick together: support and solidarity are invaluable if you're facing the full force of the law.

THE TEENAGE ACTIVISTS TAKING THE US GOVERNMENT TO COURT

In 2015, when Xiuhtezcatl Roske-Martinez was 15 years old, he decided he'd had enough. His future—and that of his entire generation—was being threatened by climate change, and someone needed to be held accountable. Now he's suing the US government, alongside a group of other young people.

In 2017, two years after filing their suit, the teens substituted Donald Trump's name for that of Obama. (As this book goes to print, their case is still ongoing.) Sometimes the only way to be heard is to take things straight to the top.

Xiuhtezcatl (pronounced "shoe-tez-cath") is still in his teens, but he's far from your average teenager. An environmental crusader with ten years' activism experience, he's also an acclaimed public speaker and an aspiring hip-hop musician who is suing the government in his spare time.

Impressively, Xiuhtezcatl is not alone in the wunderkind stakes. As Youth Director for the environmental awareness group Earth Guardians, he is one of a vast army of young activists who are shockingly confident, fearlessly outspoken, and brimming with knowledge about the state of the world. Collectively, they are fighting to change the US stance on climate change and curb the ticking time bomb of environmental chaos that their generation has been saddled with. Now he's using the law of the land in an effort to take the fight forward.

"Adults did a splendid job of messing up the planet for our generation, who now have to pick up the pieces and figure out what to do with it." Xiuhtezcatl explains. "And adults are going to be done [on this planet] a lot sooner than we are, so it's easy for them to cop out and not really think about it."

Part of the movement reached a groundbreaking pinnacle in 2015 with Xiuhtezcatl, one of 21 young activists, filing a lawsuit against the United States federal government for their lack of action. Backed up by renowned minds, including climate scientist Dr. James E. Hansen, along with the Oregon nonprofit environmental group Our Children's Trust, the lawsuit claims that the government has failed to honor its constitutional responsibility to allow children to grow up with the right to life, liberty, and property, and in a healthy atmosphere.

"The judge was incredibly intelligent and listened to everything we had to say". Xiuhtezcatl recalls. "He was very knowledgeable about the public-trust doctrine, which is one of the big doctrines that we're presenting as part of the constitution to help hold federal governments accountable."

Xiuhtezcatl has high hopes that the case will go to trial, but it's been an uphill battle for the group.

Representatives of the fossil-fuel industry filed a motion to dismiss the lawsuit in November 2015, but a federal court in Oregon ruled in favor of the young plaintiffs' "groundbreaking" action. In 2017, another attempt to have the case dismissed failed.

"The thing that's kind of scary is that if they dismiss this lawsuit, we'll have to file for an appeal, and then if the appeal is thrown out of court, then we're going to have to file another lawsuit. And the thing that sucks is that in a couple of years, things will be so bad in the climate and so much worse than they are today."

While legal counsel for the activists is provided by Our Children's Trust, the US government and the fossil-fuel industry have employed corporate giants to represent them. The imbalance would likely be even greater were the case to go to trial. But considering all that he's achieved in his years on earth, Xiuhtezcatl is fittingly nonchalant about the scale of the lawsuit. His deadpan response to possible failure? "It'd be a bummer."

"But, at the same time," he continues, "I know that we're gonna keep coming back. We're not gonna be silenced and we're not gonna quit. Our voices will continue to echo through the world and people will realize that we're serious. We're here to stay. This is not a publicity stunt, this is us fighting for our futures, in the streets and in the courts and in our communities and in our schools. We're taking the world by storm. The world ain't even ready for us."

MAKE A SCENE

A

SCENE

Pulling off a direct action

INTRODUCTION
—

Direct actions have long been a way for activists to take matters into their own hands, a chance to think outside the box while exercising the rights that generations before us fought for. Direct actions have the potential to change the game for your campaign, but finding innovative and creative ways to make the rest of us take notice—and pulling things off without a glitch—will involve a lot of hard work.

Get inspired: Direct actions from around the world

Sure, we elect our political leaders—the people who govern on our behalf. But democracy is about more than representation and elections, more than simply passing our power on to those who rule. Participating in direct actions can help us reclaim this power in its purest form.

Direct actions are all about getting out there and refusing to be silent: think strikes, think sit-ins, and think stunts. It's all about building on communal power and taking actions that, when performed individually, might go unnoticed, but when done as a collective become a force for change that's impossible to ignore.

Here are some examples to spur you into action:

1 — No more Nazis

With neo-Nazis gathering in a small German town, antifascist activists decided to play a prank that would both undermine their presence and raise money for an important cause. Unbeknown to the far-right marchers, local businesses and residents had decided to sponsor their racist walk. For every meter traveled, €10 was donated to EXIT Deutschland, a program set up to help people walk away from extremist groups.

2 — Queer Dance Party

When Donald Trump won the keys to the White House, he did so with his running mate and homophobic vice president, Mike Pence. One January night, hundreds of LGBT+ activists descended on his home in Washington, DC to, as they put it, "tell Daddy Pence: homo/transphobia is not tolerated in our country" through the medium of unapologetic and fearless dance.

3 — Taking the tarmac

In March 2017, 15 campaigners broke onto the commercial slipway at London Stansted Airport in an attempt to stop a charter flight deporting asylum seekers and refugees to Nigeria and Ghana from taking off. Using tubes and chains, the activists locked onto the plane's wheel and each other, refusing to leave until the flight was canceled. That night, the 57 people on board disembarked. Each of the activists was arrested.

4 — Critical mass

Born in San Francisco in 1992, Critical Mass protests have now taken place in hundreds of cities around the globe. As cyclists converge en masse and take over the streets of some of the world's busiest urban centers, they're riding to highlight climate change, the lack of provision for bicycles, and the need to reclaim our public spaces.

5 — Getting naked

Sometimes the simplest forms of protest are the most striking—and what takes fewer resources than stripping off? To highlight the naked greed of big pharma corporations, activists in London bared all in the windows of the London HQ of drug company Gilead.

6 — Kiss for a cause

Standing strong in the face of prejudice can be an act of defiance in and of itself. After a supermarket security guard in London told two gay men they were being "inappropriate" by holding hands, people of all genders and sexualities flocked just days later to the store for a smooch fest, proving to anyone watching that there's no shame in showing affection, whoever you are.

7 — Bridges not walls

As the world woke up to Donald Trump's inauguration as US President, activists organized across borders to say, "Build bridges, not walls." Over 250 banners were dropped from bridges across five continents, challenging Trump's divisive plans and policies with a symbol of global solidarity.

8 — Red-carpet revolt

British feminist group Sisters Uncut have a reputation for pulling off attention-grabbing direct actions that pack a punch. At the UK premiere of the blockbuster movie *Suffragette*, dozens of women staged a lie-in protest on the red carpet. As security guards dragged them away, they chanted "Dead women can't vote," highlighting cuts to domestic-violence services, which affect women the most.

JARGON BUSTER

DIRECT ACTION

A direct action can be the use of strikes, demonstration, or other forms of public protest to achieve demands outside of negotiations. But in reality it can be any form of action that seeks to achieve an immediate or direct result from an established authority or powerful institution. In other words, instead of waiting for a politician to act for you, you do it yourself.

CIVIL DISOBEDIENCE

Civil disobedience is a specific type of direct action, where activists intentionally violate laws because they believe they are unfair or unjust. Here, breaking the law is precisely the point: think Rosa Parks, who refused to give up her seat to a white man on a bus in 1950s Alabama, although the law at the time dictated that she should.

Stay alert

If you're preparing for a direct action that requires
the element of surprise, or treads a fine line
with the law, take these precautions.

Use end-to-end encrypted platforms like
WhatsApp or Signal for organizing.

Consider reaching out to a sympathetic lawyer to
discuss potential repercussions (see Chapter 6).

Turn your phones off, take out the batteries, and
leave them in a different room when you meet, just
in case someone is listening in.

Keep your e-mail and social media accounts secure
with multifactor authentication.

Only give people the details they need to know, to
limit leaks and keep information confidential.

Use a pay-as-you-go burner phone for
communications, just in case. Make sure to regularly
change numbers and buy new SIM cards, too.

Don't share pictures or videos that could
compromise the action or the people taking part.

Both in planning and execution, use code names for
one another, and for the action itself, to protect
your identities and intentions.

How to work together

Once you've agreed on a course of action, spend some time thinking carefully about every task. Of course there'll be those on the frontline taking action, but the work behind the scenes is just as important. If you have the numbers, then split up into working groups, each with a specific remit. This will ensure that your day-to-day responsibilities won't stop the job getting done.

You might want a press team, and a team in charge of legal. There should also be a group sorting out logistics, and a welfare group making sure everyone feels comfortable and safe.

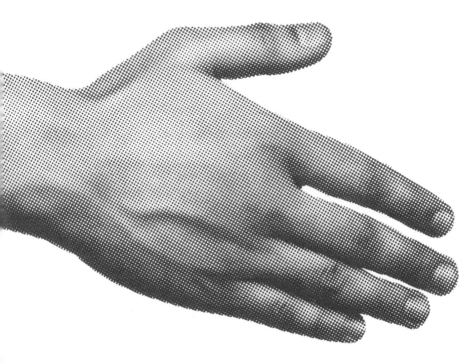

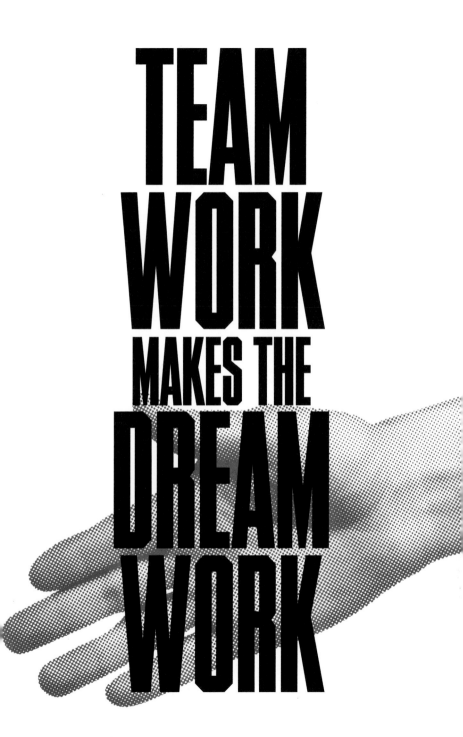

Actions have consequences

You may have the best intentions when your direct action takes off, but don't forget that when you dive in head first, the ripples can be felt by those around you.

It's all well and good to chain yourself to the front of a multinational corporation's head office, for example, but there may be low-paid workers on precarious contracts who will subsequently lose a day or more of work. Consider carefully who'll be affected by your action, and decide if it's necessary to do anything to soften the blow.

Ensure there are people on the ground not directly involved in the action, armed with flyers and open to discussion, so that people understand what you're doing and why. Be creative in your approach, from bringing coffee and snacks to starting a hardship fund for unempowered workers, such as cleaners on zero-hours contracts, who might be affected by an ongoing action.

We're all human

Committing to a direct action takes time and work, but sometimes your situation will change. Don't take on responsibilities you know you won't see through, even if you're just trying to help. There's no shame in pulling out of an action if you no longer feel safe or comfortable, either. As long as you communicate openly with your fellow activists, you can reconsider and readjust—just don't leave others in the lurch.

Nobody left behind

While civil disobedience sees activists break the law on purpose, some direct actions may also lead to arrest. We covered your legal rights in greater detail in Chapter 6, but make sure you find out where those arrested are taken for processing and interviewing. Arrestee support might be the least glamorous part of pulling off an action, but taking it in turns to wait outside the station with food, kind words, and a ride home will ensure nobody falls through the cracks.

AND REMEMBER ...

END
IT ON A H

Once the dust has settled, always have a debrief to look back on what worked and what didn't. Direct actions can be an emotional rollercoaster, especially if they last a long time or don't quite go to plan. Whatever the outcome of your action, make sure you organize a social soon after so that you can celebrate, relax, and regroup.

HOW TO MAKE YOUR ACTION IMPOSSIBLE TO IGNORE

Sometimes the old saying "Hit them where it hurts" really comes into its own. That was the thinking behind Ende Gelände ("Here and no further"), a monumental climate action that saw activists from across Europe shut down one of the continent's biggest coal mines.

It's 13 May 2016—the evening before Ende Gelände, Europe's biggest climate action for a generation. Just under 95 miles south of Berlin, the village of Proschim is a hive of activity. Activists from all across Europe are descending on this sleepy hamlet with a single goal: to shut down a lignite coal mine that, as one of the continent's dirtiest polluters, spits out an average of 3 million tons of CO_2 per year.

"I just think about the future, when I'm sat down one day with my children," says Bethan Lloyd, a 29-year-old musician from North Wales, now living in Berlin. "I imagine them asking me, 'Mum, what did you do about all this?' And I can't face the idea of telling them that I sat down quietly and did nothing."

When it comes to climate change, the facts are overwhelming: temperatures are rising, the Arctic is melting, and sea levels rose by 7.5 inches in the twentieth century. The United Nations has predicted rising temperatures will see 250 million people displaced by 2050. There is, however, a rapidly growing movement of people who refuse to be passive; people willing to put their bodies on the line in the fight against climate change.

In December 2015, world leaders met in Paris for COP21, an international climate summit tasked with halting global warming. Despite the rhetoric and the headlines, the talks were deemed a failure by many at the time: the agreement isn't legally binding, the goals have been labeled insufficient, and the proposals won't come into effect until 2020 at the earliest.

However, Melanie Mattauch, who works for 350.org, an international NGO determined to mobilize the masses to tackle climate change across the globe, remains optimistic. "The reality is, we went in not expecting anything meaningful to happen. What we wanted from Paris was for the movement to gather strength. And it happened."

In the end, nearly 3,000 people came together on 14 May in Proschim to amplify their individual voices as a single collective, intent on breaching the perimeter of the mine. At previous protests batons and teargas had been employed by heavy-handed police officers, but on this occasion the authorities held back.

For a few hours, the various groups sped across the site. Train tracks transporting coal from the mine to the power plant were blockaded, and the gigantic equipment was scaled and locked down. It was a sight to behold.

Measuring the impact of an action like this is impossible. There was certainly a real-time material impact on the planet—the coal mine was shut down for a matter of days, and coal extraction was halted. In and of itself, though, it probably didn't have a significant impact on the advance of global warming.

But it's what this action represents that truly counts. It's the coming together of people from all over a continent to stand up for a cause they believe in. It's utilizing the power of the Internet and social media to spread a message, to plan together, to turn virtual frustration into boots on the ground. It's standing up to fossil-fuel multinationals, to national governments, to those in power with so much to lose.

"As a political issue, it's clear we need an international response," says Danni Paffard, a British activist who marched on that day, highlighting that climate change is an issue that transcends national borders and requires tackling by states collectively.

"This action also provides us with an opportunity to expose ourselves to different organizing cultures, too. It helps us to innovate, to build on the social movements that came before us." Each of the activists involved took lessons home with them, and direct actions in their respective communities and countries will now benefit from the skills and contacts that they acquired.

"You can share things online, you can speak to people in person, but I don't want to have these endless conversations and not do anything," Bethan reflected as she bedded down for the night's occupation. "I wasn't in denial about climate change, but I think I denied to myself that I could do something—it felt much easier that way. Now I see that by coming together as individuals we can do something. It won't be easy, but we will be better prepared."

PLAY THE LONG GAME

You've come a long way,
but don't stop now

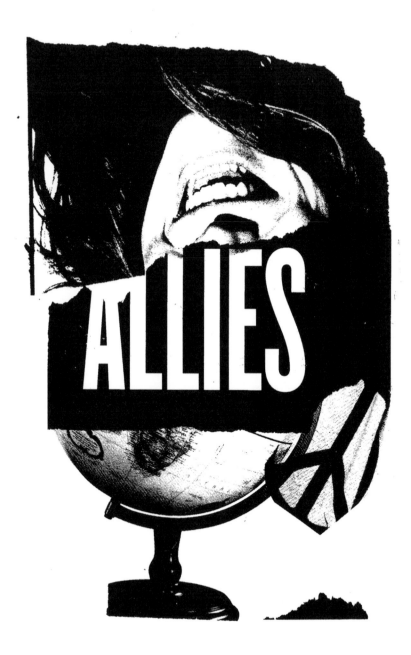

INTRODUCTION

—

There's no better feeling than realizing you have the potential to change the world, but you need to prepare for a marathon rather than a sprint. There will always be those who want to put you down, and they will always claim that you are asking for the impossible. Don't let that defeat you. Remember that you never stand alone. Above all, take care of yourself and keep focused as you go.

Link up
and learn

Whatever it is that you're fighting for, others have had similar battles before. In some cases, these will be campaigners from the past; others might be in the here and now, and perhaps just up the road.

There's no shame in seeking advice from others; sharing lessons learned is one of the greatest resources we have. Reaching out to activists locally, nationally, and across borders won't just help you understand the wider context in which you are campaigning, it will provide you with insight, guidance, and support. Even campaigns that do not relate directly to yours may have something to offer.

These relationships can soon develop into ones of mutual support: giving back and standing in solidarity with others is key. In practice this might mean attending other groups' protests, rallies, fundraisers, or direct actions. Sharing their events or activities on your group's social media is also an easy way to lend a hand.

At other times, you may wish to work closely together. Other groups may well have similar or shared objectives to that of your campaigning work, so collaborating on specific projects or actions will help widen your pool of activists while building important long-term links. Joint fundraisers might spread the burden of putting on a big event, while splitting the cost of hiring transport to attend a national demonstration can help reduce pollution.

Don't forget that support really does need to be reciprocal if you want to keep building a movement.

You're not the world's savior

It's great that you've been inspired to take on injustice, but getting all high and mighty won't do anything to further your cause. In fact, it might make you pretty unpopular in the long run. Remember that everyone is on a journey, and not every path is the same as yours.

When you interact with anyone, especially those who might be affected by the issues you've become impassioned by, don't forget you're there to support and help them. There's a mantra that you should live by: *Activism is about working with people, not for them or on their behalf*. Make sure their voices are amplified, not drowned out.

Explore your spectrum of allies

Changing the minds of people in power is one way to achieve your campaign's goals, but if history teaches us anything it's that real change comes from the ground up. Look back at our most progressive milestones—from votes for women to racial-equality legislation—and you'll see politicians playing catch up with society's hearts and minds.

An exercise known as the "Spectrum of Allies" will enable you to identify where others stand in relation to the cause you are championing—from the groups who might need a little more convincing, all the way to those who are desperate to join you.

For this exercise you need to think of society as a collection of communities, networks, and groups. Think unions, schools, subcultures, religious groups. The more precise, and the greater the number, the better. This will help you prioritize which demographics to target and identify how much work that might require.

Be careful: don't fall into the trap of only preaching to the converted or thinking of anyone who might not see eye to eye with you as a lost cause. Success will rely on shifting every group possible some way along the spectrum. It's hard work, but the payoff will be huge.

1 | Grab a large piece of paper and draw a semicircle on it. You should have an image that resembles half a pie.

2 | Write the name of your campaign underneath the straight line. Put yourself on the left side, and the opposition on the right.

3 | Split your pie into five equal slices and label them as follows:

- **Active allies**—people who agree with you and are already fighting alongside you.
- **Passive allies**—people who agree with you but right now aren't doing anything about it.
- **Neutral**—people as of yet with no opinion: unengaged, uninterested, or uninformed.
- **Passive opposition**—people who disagree with you but aren't acting on their beliefs.
- **Active opposition**—people who disagree with you and are already pushing back.

4 | Draw up a list on a separate piece of paper and list all the individuals, groups, organizations, and networks you can think of who have an opinion on your campaign. Take plenty of time, and be as specific as possible with each category. For example, rather than simply writing "young people", you might put "college students", "college students living in shared accommodation" or "college students studying maths." Don't forget to do your research and identify groups campaigning on similar issues to you who will also be able to lend you their support. The more specific you are with the characteristics you list, the more useful this exercise will be.

5 | Now take each group and place them in the appropriate pie slice. With your completed spectrum of allies you can plot out who you need to bring with you when building a coalition for change. Note down each group's contact details and make sure to get in touch.

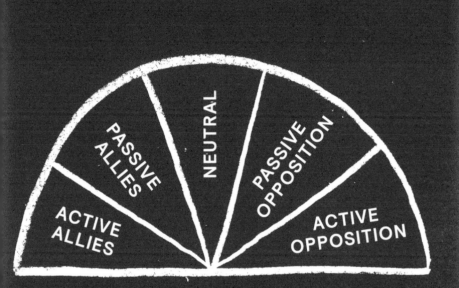

SPECTRUM OF ALLIES

JARGON BUSTER

THE OVERTON WINDOW

A term developed by Joseph P. Overton, the Overton window is a concept and tool that allows you to consider what ideas and possibilities are seen as socially acceptable by the public at large. Positions inside this symbolic window are seen as mainstream and acceptable, while the ideas that sit outside might seem radical and controversial. The most important thing to remember is that the work of activists and campaigners helps shift which ideas sit inside the window over time.

Take, for instance, same-sex marriage. One hundred years ago, homosexuality itself was criminalized, the idea of legalizing same-sex marriage wasn't considered a possibility at all. LGBT+ rights activists campaigned successfully for same-sex relationships to be decriminalized in 1967, and by 2013 same-sex marriage was legalized after gaining widespread support. Today's radicals may well be tomorrow's mainstream moderates.

What does victory look like?

Activists have a vital role in shifting public discourse. It's only through pushing the boundaries of what is possible that those in power will follow our lead. At every stage of your campaign, sit down and think hard about what constitutes a win. You may want to have a series of markers that can be seen as successes, especially if you're desperate to see more than one specific outcome.

Some campaigns will be long and drawn out, so to keep morale high, identify milestones to mark your achievements whenever you can. This will give you time to celebrate, and the drive to carry on.

Let's say your campaign's end goal is to see the decriminalization of all illegal drugs, as is the law in Portugal. You can actively campaign for this change while celebrating milestones—such as prison sentence reduction, better drugs education in schools, and increased access to harm-reduction services—along the way.

The possibilities are endless

As your campaign grows and changes, don't be afraid to think big. As you start to make headway as a movement you might find the possibilities of what you can achieve begin to grow, too. Setting out your goals is vital to tracking success and celebrating a victory, but at every juncture regroup and decide what could be next.

If your campaign is focused on a single issue—for example, stopping the closure of a local fire station because of funding cuts—keeping it open is a win. But don't let that be a limit to what you achieve. You might wish, for example, to campaign for better pay for firefighters, or start a national network of fire service campaigns.

Small change
makes change

Sometimes raising funds will be an important aspect of
your activism; in other cases it'll just be for the day-to-day
essentials. Either way, transparency is a must. If you're asking
for donations or crowdfunding, make sure you're always
upfront about where the money is going.

If you're looking to raise some serious money—let's say, to
support a community group that is strapped for cash or to
cover the travel costs of someone who would otherwise be
excluded from your work—it pays to be creative. You may want
to host an auction or fundraising night at a local venue. If you
opt to grab a bucket and take your shaking to the streets,
don't shame anyone into giving you cash. And make sure your
message is on point.

Self-care starts and ends with you ...

Throwing everything into a cause you believe in is rewarding, both for you as an activist and for the people who'll benefit from your tireless work. But you must always remember to look after yourself—it's much better to refuel at pit stops than to wait for your tank to hit empty.

Self-care is a phrase used to describe the art of looking after yourself—the methods you can employ to treat both body and mind with the same love and respect you'd give to others. There is no right way to practice self-care, but doing what is right for you sits at its heart. Here are some tips to get you started:

- **Learn to say no.** When you're overwhelmed or at capacity, saying no means saying yes to other things.
- **We all need to let our hair down.** Set aside time to socialize and unwind, both with friends and with your fellow activists.
- **Be kind to your body.** It might sound obvious, but make sure you exercise, eat well, stay hydrated, and find time to sleep.
- **We're all human.** If you're struggling, ask those around you for help. Never feel like you can't share the load.
- **Take yourself offline.** It can be a lifeline. There's no harm in switching off your phone and computer for an hour, a day, a week, or longer.

"CARING FOR YOURSELF IS NOT SELF-INDULGENCE, IT IS SELF-PRESERVATION, AND THAT IS AN ACT OF POLITICAL WARFARE."

Audre Lorde,
poet and activist

Keep your head held high

Activism is all about changing our communities for the better, but there'll be some people—usually with something to lose from the march of progress—who will try to stand in your way.

In recent years activist groups have been the target of both hostile journalists, desperate to discredit and undermine important work, and undercover police officers looking to infiltrate networks by taking advantage of people's trust.

There's no way of mitigating these risks completely, but ensuring you don't say anything in a public meeting that you wouldn't want reported on or repeated is your best shot. Protect your own social media accounts, too: some hacks will trawl through everything you've ever posted to catch you out.

If a media outlet does a hatchet job on you as an individual or a movement, demand a right of reply. It's not uncommon for newspapers and websites to print all-out lies, so a phone call to an attorney for advice might be a wise move.

As for hateful messages on Twitter: important work will always attract trolls because it challenges the status quo. Try your best to not engage, and instead throw your energy back into your campaign. Blocking abusive accounts is one way to keep your distance, but if it's necessary report abusers via the platform or even make a call to the police.

AND REMEMBER ...

THE FUTURE IS IN YOUR HA

Activism is about imagining another way of living, by fighting for something better and raising consciousness along the way. Being kind to yourself and to those around you will help ensure your activism continues long into the future. Make friends, fall in love, build communities, and create memories. There's something quite addictive about making the world a better place.

HOW BLACK LIVES MATTER BECAME A TRANSATLANTIC MOVEMENT

In an age of global activism, our struggles are no longer defined by geographical boundaries. When it comes to building a sustainable movement that matters around the world, there are lessons to be learned from activists facing similar struggles elsewhere.

Just look at Black Lives Matter, one of the defining movements of our time. What started in reaction to the loss of black lives at the hands of US police has become an international call to arms, resonating with activists in the UK and beyond.

When George Zimmerman was acquitted of the murder of 17-year-old African American Trayvon Martin back in July 2013, the verdict reeked of injustice. In cities across the United States, protestors took to the streets. Artist and activist Patrisse Cullors came up with a hashtag with two friends that would go on to become a global call to action. "Our Lives Matter, Black Lives Matter," they wrote online. Within days people were using it across the world, and now it's an international movement.

In the United States and Britain, people are dying at the hands of the police. Shared experiences of racial profiling, disproportionate deaths of black people in custody, and institutional racism have become a familiar story for citizens on both sides of the Atlantic, connecting British and American campaigners in unexpected ways.

"Those of us in the States, especially black Americans, must make more of a concerted effort to deepen our analysis and practice when it pertains to globalized anti-black racism and resistance," says Patrisse, speaking from her home in California. "Movements become global when organizers of the world unite and make clear parallels about our issues."

When people took to the streets of Ferguson, Missouri, in the wake of Mike Brown's death, it triggered a stream of direct action in England, too. Marching to the US embassy, blocking streets in the center of London, and holding "die-ins" at one of the biggest shopping malls in the UK, British activists expressed solidarity with their counterparts across the pond.

That transatlantic connection grew stronger when a delegation of British campaigners—consisting of the family members of those who have died in police custody—made their way across California, meeting activists and communities to share their stories of injustice and compare the struggles that their communities face.

"Going to the US allowed me to bridge the gaps we haven't been able to before," explains Kadisha Brown-Burrell, whose brother Kingsley died in 2011 after an interaction with some officers in the West Midlands. "Linking with campaigners and family members and organizations alike gave us that link in order to move forward in Britain."

As the families shared stories, they realized their experiences were alarmingly similar. "It's no coincidence," adds Marcia Rigg, whose brother Sean died after contact with police in South London back in 2008. "It's deliberate. The UK and US are close, so this just highlights the institutional and systemic failings that are mirrored across borders."

Years later, and Marcia still has questions but few answers. "What's happening today is modern-day slavery. Nothing has changed. We aren't chained but we are handcuffed; not lynched from a tree but killed by police," she says. "There is change coming from the movements in the US, so in order to adapt with those movements, we need to join forces."

At meetings and rallies throughout the trip, all kinds of practical lessons were exchanged, including one particularly hands-on tool. The Mobile Justice App allows witnesses of police violence to upload footage in real time to a secure server. Developed by the American Civil Liberties Union, it's facilitating citizen "policing of the police" and was a standout takeaway for British campaigners. Some lessons, though, will take a little longer to incorporate, including learning from how different responses to police and state violence have panned out.

On 4 August 2011, 29-year-old Mark Duggan was shot dead by the Metropolitan Police in London, sparking uprisings across the country. But the discontent quickly dissipated. The justice system came down hard and the narrative formed that this was nothing but "mindless violence."

Yet in Ferguson, things were different. The uprisings have been accepted as social protests. Patrisse Cullors believes that taking to social media allowed people on the streets to control the debate. "Social media provides a platform that allowed us to be and go global, but more importantly allows us to raise the levels of consciousness in our communities, and then make these very important connections."

It's also the sustained nature of the movement in the US that has contributed to its success; people took to the streets, and they stayed there—a lesson the British activists are keen to bring back home. In the struggle for equality and liberation for black people, building bridges internationally is vital.

"WHAT CO
IS NOT THE M
WE LIVED. IT IS
WE HAVE MADE
OTHERS THAT
THE SIGNIFI
LIFE W

TS IN LIFE
E FACT THAT
E DIFFERENCE
THE LIVES OF
LL DETERMINE
NCE OF THE
EAD."

Nelson Mandela

FURTHER READING
—

Aftershock: Confronting Trauma in a Violent World
pattrice jones (2007)

The Autobiography of Malcolm X
Alex Haley and Malcolm X (1965)

Beautiful Trouble: A Toolbox for Revolution
Andrew Boyd and Dave Oswald Mitchell (2012)

Don't Think of an Elephant! Know Your Values and Frame the Debate
George Lakoff (2004)

Feminism is for Everybody
bell hooks (2000)

*Freedom is a Constant Struggle: Ferguson, Palestine,
and the Foundation of a Movement*
Angela Y. Davis (2015)

From #blacklivesmatter To Black Liberation
Keeanga-Yamahtta Taylor (2016)

Hope in the Dark: Untold Histories, Wild Possibilities
Rebecca Solnit (2004)

Pedagogy of the Oppressed
Paulo Freire (1970)

The Protest Handbook
Tom Wainwright, Anna Morris, Katherine Craig, and Owen Greenhall (2012)

This Changes Everything: Capitalism vs the Climate
Naomi Klein (2014)

USEFUL ORGANIZATIONS

American Civil Liberties Union (ACLU)—
Founded in 1920, the ACLU is a not-
for-profit group that works to defend
and preserve the individual rights and
liberties guaranteed by the Constitution
and laws of the United States. Speak to
them if you feel your rights have been
violated.

Amnesty International—Investigating
and exposing abuses for over 50 years,
Amnesty is the world's largest grassroots
human rights movement, with over 7
million members.

Friends of the Earth—Originally founded
as an anti-nuclear group in 1969, Friends
of the Earth are an invaluable resource if
you're involved in environmental activism.

Greenpeace—Founded in Canada in
1971, Greenpeace is a leading voice on
environmental issues and climate change.
There are opportunities to be involved
with their work across the globe.

Human Rights Watch (HRW)—
HRW are an international
nongovernmental organization
researching and campaigning on
human rights. Hit them up for advice
and campaigning opportunities.

**National Association for the
Advancement of Colored People
(NAACP)—**The NAACP's mission is to
eliminate race-based discrimination in the
United States. They have a long history of
using activism, lobbying, education, and
campaigning to achieve this goal.

National Lawyers Guild (NLG)—With
chapters across the United States, the
NLG is a public interest association of
lawyers, law students, paralegals, and
other activist legal workers. Much of
their work is dedicated to providing
legal advice and support to activists
on the ground.

National Organization for Women (NOW)—
Founded in 1966, NOW is the largest
organization of feminist grassroots
activists in the United States. Its mission
is to eliminate discrimination and secure
the equal rights of all women and girls
in every area of social, political, and
economic life.

ACKNOWLEDGMENTS
—

Without the wealth of expertise, guidance, and knowledge of an incredible team of people, this book would never have been completed: Andrea Kurland, Clive Wilson, Chelsea Edwards, Dominique Sisley, Amelia Abraham, Adam White, Richard Power Sayeed, Joseph Alloway, Joe Ryle, Hannah Elsisi, Ben Smoke, Lyndsay Burtonshaw, Ellie Mae O'Hagan, James Robertson, Jessie Seal, Josie Long, Malia Bouattia, Jude Bunting, Ravi Naik, Simon Natas, Tom Wainwright, Dan Glass, Andrea Cornwall, Adriana Swain, Georgia Whitaker Hughes, Ashley Joiner, John Parton, Marc Valli, Vince Medeiros, Wendy Klerck, Taryn Paterson, and Alex Wade.

PHOTOGRAPHY

© Alejandro Alvarez, page 161; © Chris Bethell, page 164; © Rob Gilbert, page 162; © Jonathan Hanson, pages 200, 203; © Seb Heseltine, page 162; © Jade Jackman, pages 161, 163; © Mario Jean, pages 108, 111; © Theo McInnes, pages 56, 59, 86, 89, 160, 164, 176, 179; © David O'Connor, pages 36, 39; © Andrew White, page 152; © Sye Williams, pages 126, 129; © Earth Guardians, page 155.

Oliver Stafford, designer of this book, is Art Director at *Huck* and an illustrator and designer for iconic movie magazine, *Little White Lies*.

Huck is a premium youth culture channel across video, digital, and print. Offering a powerful alternative to mainstream media, *Huck* roams the globe to document counterculture as it unfolds. ***huckmagazine.com***